THE BEST MEN'S MONOLOGUES FROM NEW PLAYS, 2019

THE BEST MEN'S MONOLOGUES FROM NEW PLAYS, 2019

EDITED AND WITH AN INTRODUCTION BY LAWRENCE HARBISON

APPLAUSE
THEATRE & CINEMA BOOKS
Guilford, Connecticut

Published by Applause Theatre & Cinema Books
An imprint of The Rowman & Littlefield Publishing Group, Inc.
4501 Forbes Blvd., Ste. 200
Lanham, MD 20706
www.rowman.com

Distributed by NATIONAL BOOK NETWORK

British Library Cataloguing in Publication Information Available

Library of Congress Cataloging-in-Publication Data

ISBN 978-1-4930-5329-2 (pbk. : alk. paper)
ISBN 978-1-4930-5330-8 (electronic)

♾️™ The paper used in this publication meets the minimum requirements of American National Standard for Information Sciences—Permanence of Paper for Printed Library Materials, ANSI/NISO Z39.48-1992.

CONTENTS

INTRODUCTION

Here you will find a rich and varied selection of monologues for men, most of which are from plays of recent vintage, many of them produced and/or published in the 2018–2019 theatrical season. Many are for younger performers (teens through 30s), but there are some excellent pieces for older men as well. The age of the character is indicated in each monologue, but you will find that many may be done by actors of different ages. Some are comic (laughs), some are dramatic (generally, no laughs), some are seriocomic (some laughs). Some are rather short and some are rather long. All represent the best in contemporary playwriting.

Several of the monologues are by playwrights whose work may be familiar to you, such as Don Nigro, Theresa Rebeck, Steven Levenson, Brooke Berman, Richard Vetere, Jack Gilhooley, Len Jenkin, Sam Bobrick, Anna Ziegler, Lloyd Suh, and Aaron Posner (the latter three of whom I interviewed for my book *How I Did It: Establishing a Playwriting Career* [Applause Theatre & Cinema Books]); others are by exciting up-and-comers such as C. S. Hanson, Merredith Allen, Max Baker, Eric John Meyer, Lia Romeo, and Cary Gitter. Many of the plays from which these monologues have been culled have been published, and hence are readily available either from the publisher/licensor or from a theatrical bookstore such as the Drama Book Shop in New York. Some may not be published for a while, in which case you may contact the author or agent to request a copy of the entire text of the play containing the monologue that suits your fancy. Information on publishers/rights holders may be found in the Rights and Permissions section in the back of this anthology.

Break a leg in that audition! Knock 'em dead in class!

Lawrence Harbison

P.S. Although each monologue lists the character's age, many would work perfectly well for an actor of a different age.

AFTER

Michael McKeever

Dramatic
ALAN BECKMAN, 40s–50s

ALAN BECKMAN, *a grieving father, tries to explain why his son took a gun to school, two years prior, to the father of the boy who took the gun away from him and killed him.*

ALAN   Perception versus reality. The threat—the perception of danger—was so strong, that his *instincts* overrode common sense. Because perception is based on instinct. And instinct is what keeps us alive. [*Beat.*] Your son is a bully. He had no other choice. There's a German word. A chess term. *Zugzwang.* It's when you make a move that you don't want to make—a move you're forced to make—when you have no other options left. *Zugzwang.* [*Beat.*] I told him he had to be a man. The day before. Of course, I had no idea what was really happening. I . . . [*Beat.*] I told him the world didn't tolerate cowards. The only way to deal with any situation is to face it head on. I told him he had to be a man. [*Beat.*] Even now, I want so much to hate your son. I want so much to hate you. I just don't have the strength any more. There's a pain. It's everywhere. It starts in your soul and radiates out. I keep thinking it's going to stop, but it doesn't. [*Beat.*] People mean well. They tell you they love you and they send their prayers and after a while, you just want to scream *keep your goddamn prayers, I don't want them. They don't help.* And one day bleeds into the next. And you think, maybe today is the day it stops hurting. But it doesn't. [*Beat.*] In the two years since Matty, there's been what, sixty-two school shootings? How is that even possible? And I know what those parents are going through. I understand what they're feeling. And part of me wants to reach out to them, but the reality is that

1

all I really feel is "Good. Now you know what this is like, too."
And then it's one day past, and then two, and then a week,
and the news cameras go home, and the talking heads on TV
start talking about something else. And before you know it,
it's done. It's over with. It's a footnote. [*Beat.*] He's a footnote.
[*Beat.*] But the pain never stops. [*Beat.*] It's funny, nobody
talks about what happens after. After all the attention has
died down. When the world goes back to not caring. No one
considers you or the life you're supposed to live after.

AMERICAN SON

Christopher Demos-Brown

Dramatic
STOKES, late 40s–60, African American

STOKES *is the night shift supervisor at a police station. He is talking to* KENDRA, *an African American woman whose son, Jamal, is missing. Her estranged husband,* SCOTT *(who is white) has just lost control and shoved the police officer who has been trying to figure out what has happened to Jamal, and then resisted arrest.* STOKES *and the other officer have handcuffed* SCOTT, *and the other officer has taken him away to book him.* KENDRA *has called* STOKES *an Uncle Tom.*

STOKES   I'll tell ya—two minutes with you, I know your whole adult life. I know you got a husband carries around a picture of you on his phone. Every time he say some fool ass racist thing, he pull up that picture and go

[*Pretending to hold up a picture on a phone.*]

"Oh no. Not me. 'Cause looky here at my Black wife." [*Beat.*] I know how you could never explain to him that pain in your heart . . . That pain that claws out your contentment 'cause every public service announcement for hepatitis C and every malt liquor billboard got someone who looks like your baby boy in it. Or why your son was the tallest, smartest kid in the third grade but the teacher never seemed to call on him no matter how high he raised his l'il brown hand. 'Cause that's a pain your man could never quite understand. So you tried to kill that pain by making your son "proud" and telling him to live the "American Dream." Teaching him to "assert his rights" instead of how to survive as a Black man in this country. One thing I know for sure about this incident already. Just like almost every other one of 'em: If the young brothers woulda just shut their mouths and done what they were told, none of us would be here tonight. That's what I suggest you do— sit tight and shut up.

[*He turns to go.*]

Oh. And sistah . . . Next time you call a Black man a Tom? It'd play a whole lot better if that Black man didn't just drag your *White* husband out the room in handcuffs.

ANARCHY

Don Nigro

Dramatic
SACCO, 30s

In the 1920s, SACCO, an Italian immigrant and an anarchist, is in prison awaiting execution for murders he and his friend VANZETTI insist they did not commit. He is trying to explain to the journalist JOHN RHYS PENDRAGON why he initially lied to the police about what he was up to at the time of the robbery in which the murders were committed. He is passionate, angry, and, whatever else he might have done, the victim of highly unjust and deeply prejudiced legal system. He has a young wife and children and knows he is soon going to be executed.

SACCO   Do you know about what they do to my friend Salsedo? A good man. An anarchist, like me. A decent man. He always told the truth. It was a matter of honor with him. So they pick him up for questioning. No particular crime. They say on suspicion he's been involved in radical activities. That means being Italian in the wrong neighborhood. It means anything they don't like. They take my friend Salsedo up to the top floor of a building one night. In the morning, girls going to work find Salsedo's body on the sidewalk, his brains splattered out like a rose. This was a man who never in his life committed no crime except to use his brain to think a little bit different than the people in charge, so they throw him out a seven story window. They say he must have slipped, maybe he try to flap his arms and fly home to Italy, because everybody knows Italians are all crazy. This is what they do to my friend Salsedo, who always told the truth. They say his crime was having radical literature. Books. My friend had books. His crime was, he had books. What kind of a country is it where they kill you because you have books? We got all these books and pamphlets, that we give to people, to teach them about our cause. But when we hear what they did to Salsedo, we think we better get rid of these things, or they kill us, too. But there's a lot, so we need a car to go and dump them someplace, and this man Boda has a car. So we go to the garage to get the car, but the lady say the car ain't ready, we got to come back later. And on the streetcar, coming home, the police arrest Vanzetti and me. Now, what are we supposed to do? They throw a man out a window just for having the sort of books we're trying to get rid of. So we supposed to tell the police that's what we want the car for? What are we supposed to say to them? We supposed to tell them the names of our friends so they can throw them out windows, too?

ANARCHY

Don Nigro

Dramatic
VANZETTI, 40s

In the 1920s, VANZETTI is an Italian immigrant, an anarchist, who with his friend SACCO has been sentenced to be electrocuted for murders he insists they did not commit, after a trial presided over by a highly prejudiced judge. Now he is in prison awaiting his execution. He is a quiet, apparently gentle man who loves to read, and here he tells the journalist JOHN RHYS PENDRAGON and Pendragon's young daughter, ANNE, about his attempts to understand America and why Americans seem so desperate to kill him.

VANZETTI   I been reading American history. In America, you got the Puritans and the Pioneers. The Puritans, they think having money means God loves you. You got no money, it's your fault, you get what you deserve. Puritans like to be above and look down their nose. Now, a Pioneer, that's different. He's a Puritan with no money. The Puritans, they spit on him and cheat him, look down their nose at him, so he goes West and kills Indians and steals their land, then cuts down all the trees and rapes the land so nothing grows there no more. The Pioneers say, God gives you what you take. Everything is here for us to take and use and kill. God put it here for that. But your Puritans and your Pioneers they agree about some things, like art, for example. For both your Puritans and your Pioneers, art is something which is at best a hobby to waste your time with when you're not doing something important, like killing people or stealing their land or jacking up the rent, but at worst, art is a terrible thing, will corrupt their children, because art is a thing that asks questions, art is an investigation into truth, and these people sure they already got the truth, and the only kind of exploration they like is the kind makes money and kills people. Conquest. They want to control everything you read and say and hear and think, because they know God is on their side. And if you're different, if you look different or talk different or think different or ask questions, they make a nice speech about what a great country it is and then they kill you. You can learn a lot about America if you study history. They want to kill us because we're Italians. We like art. We like nature. We like women. We like to talk and argue and trade ideas, investigate the world, ask questions all the time. Why this? How come that? They got to kill us. They got no other choice. In America they got no questions. Just answers.

ANARCHY

Don Nigro

Dramatic
JUDGE THAYER, 70

In the 1920s, JUDGE THAYER *has just presided over the murder trial of the anarchists* SACCO *and* VANZETTI *and sentenced them to death. Here* SACCO's *young wife has sought out the judge in his garden and begged him to spare her husband's life. The judge is not a fan of immigrants, has presided over an extremely unfair trial, and is refusing to grant a retrial despite new evidence that might exonerate her husband.*

JUDGE THAYER   Evil. You want to know what evil is? Evil is disorder. Evil is chaos. Evil is anarchy. It's all fine and good to talk about the natural state of mankind, like your husband does, but look at this. This is the natural state. That snake over there, swallowing the children of the field mouse. That praying mantis making a nice lunch out of a grasshopper. These weeds, which, if I let them grow, would take over this garden in a matter of days and strangle everything here. They would overwhelm the flowers and the tomatoes and in no time at all there'd be no beauty and nothing to eat. The snakes and the spiders and the weeds and the poison ivy and the rabbits and stray dogs would entirely devour this garden, if it were not for me, if it were not for my constant vigilance. I preserve order here so that my children can eat the fruit of this garden. I scare away the crows and kill the weeds and keep things pruned. I poison the gophers and shoot the rabbits. I am all that stands between this garden and the horrors of the natural world. And I am all that stands between your children, the safety of your children, and the natural anarchy of the world, the cannibalistic, bomb-throwing, chaos-loving anarchy which your stupid and hypocritical husband believes in so deeply he went out and murdered two innocent men with families of their own to get money to buy more bombs. Well, you're damned lucky I'm here, Mrs. Sacco, and so are your children. Because in a world run by people like your husband, those children would most likely already be dead by now. So get out of my sight and let me tend my garden. You are an entirely imaginary personage and I am not speaking to you, because if I was speaking to you, I'd be forced to have you arrested, and then who would take care of your children? You see that I am not without compassion. If I were not the God of this garden, then your children would be devoured by jackals. You see that front porch there? Sitting on that front porch, on a lazy summer afternoon, swinging on the swing, drinking lemonade. A sleepy old dog. Kids screaming at the swimming hole. That's America. That's what I want to save. And if some bunch of damned half-educated greasy spaghetti-bending wops want to destroy that, I'll do anything to save it. Anything. Now you want to blow yourself up, you go right ahead. Just don't trample on my gladiolus. Just take them damned children and go back to whatever damned filthy sewer you crawled out of. Because this is the land of the free and the home of the brave. It's not a damned dumping ground for all the criminals and psychopaths in Europe. And if you ever set foot on my property again, I'll make sure you never see those children of yours again. Capeesh?

ANARCHY

Don Nigro

Dramatic
MORELLI, 30

In the 1920s, MORELLI *is a gangster, in prison for armed robbery, and the journalist* JOHN RHYS PENDRAGON *has received information that it is in fact the Morelli gang that has committed the murders for which* SACCO *and* VANZETTI *are about to be executed. In a desperate last-minute attempt to save their lives,* RHYS *has gone to* MORELLI *and asked him what the truth is. But* MORELLI *is not interested in the truth. Here he reveals to* RHYS *his contempt for journalism, the truth, and anarchy. He considers himself a good, patriotic American businessman who just now and then might happen to have to kill people in the course of business.*

MORELLI   Maybe you want the truth so you can sell a few more fucking newspapers with it, but let me tell you, the cops, that prick judge, the prosecutor, them people don't want the truth. They'd probably give me a better deal to keep my damned mouth shut. If the Virgin Mary came down from Heaven and wrote the truth on their dicks they wouldn't believe it. And if they did believe it, it still wouldn't make any difference. They got to kill them boys. What I say about anything ain't gonna matter to them. They're a couple of fucking anarchists, for Christ's sake. Look, I'm a good American. I work for a living. I got my own business. America is built of business. These two characters are just a couple of jerks. I'm the kind of guy America is made of. America runs on my kind of person. But these guys, they come over here, it ain't like they thought it would be, right away they want to change everything. They think if they just get rid of the government, everything will be great. That's the stupidest fucking thing I ever heard. What the hell do they think people are, anyway?

You do away with the government, in six weeks people are gonna be eating each other on Second Avenue. People are not rational and they are not good. People are cannibals. They're sheep, and they're cannibals. People are cannibalistic sheep, and governments know that, and business men like me know that, and we all work together for the good of humanity. I'm just a guy trying to make a living. But these anarchist assholes, they give us Italians a bad name. They don't believe in authority. I believe in authority. I been paying off cops and politicians my whole life. Without somebody in authority, who would we bribe? And these dumb anarchist sons of bitches don't believe in God. I believe in God. I go to mass every day, when I can. God helps those that help themselves. God helps the strong. The weak can get their reward in Heaven.

THE ANTELOPE PARTY

Eric John Meyer

Comic
BEN, late 20s–early 30s

BEN *is hosting a gathering of Brony friends at his apartment (Bronies are adult fans of the children's cartoon* My Little Pony*) and sharing his feelings about being misunderstood in a community where anyone who is different gets bullied.*

BEN   I'm trying to work on that color in my rainbow—listening more, talking less. I don't want to be un-Generous. Does anyone mind if I go next, by the way? Cool, thanks. It's just that when we're all here together and my apartment transforms into Equestria, I get excited. And I have a lot of things to say. Which is why I love to play Fluttershy, because once I've expressed myself with words in The Circle, she allows me to express my inner silence. Jean, you'll see what I mean when we get started. And Shawn, I'm really glad you brought up going incognito, because that's what I've been thinking about this week—how frustrating it is to have to do it. I mean, I know it's necessary these days, but like, why should it have to be? Why should it be that if I show up dressed a little different than you're used to, you're not gonna serve me at your restaurant? Or I'm gonna have to be afraid of some pack of dudes coming home from a bar? And I'm not defending those Neighborhood Watch guys either. I mean, a bunch of assholes in matching trucker hats don't exactly make me feel safer. To be honest, they'd be scary if they weren't so ridiculous. But still—why should we have to play by everyone else's rules? We're not hurting anyone. But then people who have no idea what the show's about are judging us and calling us freaks??

ASKING FOR IT
Molly Goforth

Seriocomic
DONALD, mid 30s–early 40s

DONALD *is on his cell phone, via Bluetooth.*

DONALD   What I'm . . . what I'm . . . Excuse me, I'm talking here
. . . what I'm telling you is that I'm holding the warranty in
my hand and it says it expires at . . . but it doesn't *say* BUT
IT DOESN'T *SAY* Eastern Standard time so you cannot hold
me to that . . . don't "policy" me, I know what policy means,
I make up policy out of my Alpha Bits in the morning so
don't you try to pawn that off on me, I'm not some goddam
plebiscite with a fucking Discover card, you can goddam well
change your policy . . . my secretary DID call you three times
about this in the past week, so we did contact you before the
deadline regardless of the time zone and no one ever called
us back! You don't? Oh, my gosh, is that right? Well, I'll tell
you what, *Chantal*, this isn't the Smooth FM goddam Midnight Request Hour and I've got a sneaking suspicion that
you weren't groomed for your nine-fifty-an-hour customer
dis-service position inside the limestone walls of a Pyrenees
convent, so . . . what I *mean* that I'm sure you've not only
heard worse, I'm sure you *use* worse language on a daily
basis hauling your half-dozen brats to the Head Start Free
Breakfast Program while screaming at their baby daddies
on the walkie-talkie feature of your no-credit-check cell
phone, so don't pull the shrinking violet act on me. I've got
a goddam Rascal 600T motorized scooter that needs a drive
belt, and I want it fucking FedExed to me *yesterday*, Chantal,
do you *feel* me? I want to hang up this phone to answer the
doorbell and I want my goddam doorman Gokchen to be
standing there with a drive belt from you that's been sitting

in my lobby for two days because Gokchen has been so tanked on hashish since his wife went back to Ankara with the baby that he has to be restrained from pissing in the fucking potted plumeria. Okay? So if you want to know what you can do for me at this point, what you can do is *turn back time* and send me my fucking drive belt *three days ago* when I first called. You think about that for a sec while I take this call.

ATLAS PIT
Alex Paul Burkart

Dramatic
NORM, 50

After OZZY's girlfriend dies in a tragic accident, he runs away from home, shuts himself up within a seedy apartment flat, and becomes drug addicted. In this monologue, OZZY's father, NORM, who has arrived at his son's apartment, tries to pull his son out of a tragic downward spiral using his own haunting past as a tactic to demonstrate the everlasting obstacles one must overcome to continue to live.

NORM   When I was ten years old I knocked over a glass of milk at the supper table and my father took me out to the garage and laid a leather strap across my ass. When I was twelve he upgraded it to one of his golf clubs. He used to beat me until I could barely walk, then he'd lock me inside the garage and leave me there like a sick dog for the rest of the night. Gave me newspapers to piss on. I stole a bottle of whiskey and kept it in a shoebox behind a loose board in the wall. After he beat me, I would drink. When I ran out of whiskey I stole more. I kept stealing until Mr. Ballinger, who ran the liquor market, caught me and called my ol' man. Since I wasn't allowed in the liquor store any longer, I started drinking mouthwash. Got so fucked up your grandmother found me throwing up blood in the bathroom, had to rush me to the ER where they found all the bruises and busted up bones and shit that I had been sentenced to. My mother left that man. That lousy excuse for a father. She took me here. To escape. But that need for removal has followed me like a fucking curse. There isn't a day when I don't think about how much I could use a drink. But I fight it. I fight it like my life depends on it. Because it does.

ATLAS PIT

Alex Paul Burkart

Dramatic
OZZY, 17–18

As OZZY revisits an old gravel quarry turned pond at night, an onlooking stranger appears, offering him a drug that brings users so close to death that they "see those waiting on the other side." OZZY, who has already barely survived previous experimentation with the drug, reveals to the stranger a tragedy that happened at this very location—a tragedy that caused an emptiness that cursed him into an everlasting addiction to the past.

OZZY   She drowned. Right here in the pit. We were having a fight. Over this shit actually, before I even knew what it was. She jumped in to get away from me, and never came back up. I tried to get her out, but my feet just kept slipping on the rocks below. The drop is so steep. It's not a real pond you know? This place. It's an old gravel pit that happened to have a water spring under it. The drop is almost straight down . . . Anyway, I couldn't get her in time. I tried—but it was too late . . .

Best reason they could give for it all was sudden body cramping. An anomaly. Her muscles just had tightened up so much that they stopped working. Bound her like ropes. [*Slight pause.*] She was the captain of the swim team. Fastest backstroke in the state. How does a state champion swimmer drown in a goddamned pond?! [*Beat.*] Sometimes I like to just come up here and sit. Tinker around on the guitar, read, remember. Whatever I feel like doing. I think that can be more powerful than anything, you know? Just living. And there is something about this place. I can't exactly pinpoint what it is—but there is something about it. It doesn't scare me, it calms me. Maybe because it reminds me of her—she loved it here so much . . . I still miss her a lot, you know. There is still this like emptiness inside of me. I tried to fill it with my family, and helping with my brother and all, but it doesn't help. I guess I need to embrace that it'll never go away. Sucks, but at least I know it's the truth.

AT ST. WILDING'S
Monica Raymond

Dramatic
NICHOLAS DEMPSEY, late 40s

An alumnus of a boys' prep school confronts the headmaster about the abuse he suffered when he was a student there thirty years ago.

NICHOLAS   Dr. Dakin, spare me your niceties. I didn't come to wax nostalgic over rolling hills, honor codes, hearts and minds. I'm not your donor. To me, Wilding's the place I was abused. Can you hear that? Or have you swallowed the shit of your own brochures? This is no joke! Please don't make light of it. I was abused here, can you understand? And nothing that I see in your demeanor shows anything has changed. That maggot's still babbling *"arma virumque cano"*—I guarantee he's ogling some young man, even as we sit here. Hand on your thigh, hand on your thigh—I know it sounds like nothing, but you know the swim team was the thing I loved the best, and that still haunts me—what if I'd kept swimming? I was good, really good, I won the prize in sophomore year, in junior year I quit—Didn't that give you pause? You never wondered why a natural athlete in a sport he flourished in, why would he quit like that? Now every time there's something that I love, I drop it as I feel it's getting good. It's women, jobs. I'm dogged by those gray eyes and creeping hands—it's rape, not rape but somehow worse than rape, rape you can say is something. But this, why you can always say, "it's nothing."

AT THE TABLE

Michael Perlman

Dramatic
ELLIOT, mid-30s, white, gay

ELLIOT *is speaking to* NICHOLAS, *also mid-30s, black, gay.* ELLIOT
and NICHOLAS's *mutual friend has been not-so-subtly trying to set
them up during a weekend trip with their friends. A few arguments
break out among* ELLIOT *and his other friends, fueled by alcohol
and pot.* NICHOLAS *witnesses* ELLIOT *saying some things he may
soon regret, and* ELLIOT *tries to convince* NICHOLAS *that he's not
who he may be appearing to be this weekend. Except . . . isn't he
exactly that person?*

ELLIOT I mean . . . I'm really a happy person. [*Beat.*] I think.
[*Beat.*] I mean. Who's happy, really, right? Who our age at
least? I mean, all life is is a series of . . . ways in which we've
disappointed—well, ourselves really. All we do is follow our
passions. Follow our—I don't know—a path. Follow a path.
Not even following. Being driven down. Being driven down a
path. And not even backseat drivers. We just end up places.
And it's like—you know, it's like—when we're little . . . When
we're little. When we're little, anything can happen. I could
. . . I mean, I wanted to be my parents, right? Have a—well
when I was really little—a wife. And, you know, family. And
you know—my parents were twenty-three when they got
married. They were twenty-six when I was born. Twenty-six.
And you can, like, catch up in your career. You can't catch up
in life. You can't . . . I don't know. And I'm happy. I think. I, you
know, I love my friends. You can't see it today, I know. I don't
know—I can't see it today I guess. But I love my friends—
they're the best, aren't they? They're the best. I think. I don't
know. Maybe they're not. Maybe I'm just friends with them
because we're friends. Like, maybe that's just . . . It's just, like,

again—am I just like friends with them cause they're in the car? I don't know. Maybe our lives are just, like, already, like—the road is already there. Like, fate. But I don't believe in fate. I don't think. I, like, believe that you have to, you know, make the life you want to happen . . . happen. But then I just, you know, follow the path. So who is me? Which one is essentially me, you know? I don't know who I essentially am. I don't. Yeah. I don't know. [*Beat.*] But I think I'm happy.

BABEL

Jacqueline Goldfinger

Seriocomic
STORK, any age

The STORK *is a bird, the type of bird associated with pregnancy and infancy. He might have a raspy voice like Harvey Fierstein. He is speaking to a friend, trying to convince her to undergo a difficult medical procedure.*

STORK   Maximilian the Stork the Sixth. Was a fine stork. Long elegant legs. A beak that couldn't be beat. Every baby wanted to be carried by him. He would wrap them so gently in silk fabric—in the color of their choosing, none of that pink/blue gender stereotype bullshit. But he had an undiagnosed heart condition. And when they finally discovered it, it was too late. Too far gone to fix it. But he wouldn't stop. Carrying babies in handkerchiefs and looking ridiculous was his favorite thing to do. And he felt strong, and sure, no matter what the doctors said. And one night, when he's carrying one of those kids over the ocean, his heart condition kicked in. And his heart stopped. And he dropped that baby into the ocean. It drowned. Then he dropped into the ocean after it. And he drowned. Two lives, gone. Like that. When they pulled the baby's body out of the water, it was still clutching its pacifier in its hand, and its mouth was open, like it was still screaming. For life. For a future it would never have, due to Grandpop's heart condition. Screaming for its mother, whom it would never suckle, and her partner, whom it would never meet. . . . So think about that. Think about, you don't want to do the certification. You want to take on society? You want to take on nature and nurture and the fucking genetic code itself? Go broke trying to get certified after the kid is born? You may not just be killing your baby.

You may be killing someone else's. We gotta get the bad shit out of our genes man. The heart conditions, the behavioral conditions, the, whatever it happens to be. Get it gone. This is the only way.

BERNHARDT/HAMLET
Theresa Rebeck

Dramatic
EDMOND ROSTAND, 41

SARAH BERNHARDT, *the greatest actress of her day, is presenting a production of Hamlet—with herself in the title role. The great playwright* EDMOND ROSTAND *has ended their affair and gone back to his wife. But there he is, standing before her. She has asked him why he has come back.*

EDMOND   I am here because I cannot seem to survive away from you. I told myself I could, I must, I can live on memory, I can hoard the smell of you in a handkerchief I stole from your boudoir six months ago, sorry, I can read and read again the words I wrote for you, and your voice is there but it is an echo, or worse, a fabrication. It is not you. It is only a dream of you, and I am not alive, anywhere. Anywhere but here! I cannot separate what you are and what I am one from the other anymore. How many times have I watched you, standing out here alone knowing that it is my words you say, while they are hanging on your lips and your looks, it is my heart beating, it is my will, and soul, it is I who have taken years of my life to write our masterpiece only to disappear into the silence behind you. Away from you, I am nothing; I am a wraith in a dark wind. The only time I am fully alive is when I see you here, on the stage, launching yourself into eternity. But then it all comes back, my life, life itself, comes, in a rush that is so powerful I fear it might destroy me. And yet, there is no place for me here now. I cannot, I cannot be a part of any of this. I do not know what I want, beyond the wanting of you. What is a playwright, what are words, without a voice? What am I, without you? Before you, what was I? I did not come here to frighten you. Frighten you? You fear nothing. Doubt thou the stars are fire; Doubt that the sun doth move; Doubt truth to be liar; But never doubt I love.

BERNHARDT/HAMLET
Theresa Rebeck

Dramatic
EDMOND ROSTAND, 41

SARAH BERNHARDT, *the greatest actress of her time, is presenting Hamlet—with herself in the title role. It is a Herculean task for any actor, but she has found the language to be poetically dense and difficult. She has asked her lover, the great playwright* EDMOND ROSTAND, *to do an adaptation in order to make Hamlet more play-able for her. He has come to her to tell her that he has given up—he cannot do it.*

EDMOND   If anyone is being used up in this agreement—it is me. You tell me that I am the greatest playwright of our time and then you want me to take whatever gifts I have and and and annihilate them in service to your demented idea—That to make you a decent Hamlet we must destroy him. And destroy me in the doing. You have consigned me to the worst prison of any imagination, I could be bounded in a nutshell and count myself king of infinite space were it not that I have bad dreams about what a terrible writer I am next to Shakespeare. It is hell living in his mighty head. It is hell thinking that my greatest achievement next to Hamlet is nothing. And you put me there. Everyday. Everyday, I stare at the most beautiful writing the world has seen. Is likely to see. Ever. And you ask me to destroy it. For you! For my love of you. And for your ego! For your fear! And I cannot use my gift for any of it. I cannot do it.

BETWEEN HERE AND DEAD

Merridith Allen

Dramatic
MICHAEL, 20s

MICHAEL *has always dreamed of building a better life for himself
and his girlfriend,* CAROL. *But he always seems to go about it the
wrong way. Facing a prison sentence for trying to cover up a murder,*
MICHAEL *is terrified he's going to lose his best friend, his girlfriend,
and possibly himself.*

MICHAEL   DO NOT DO THIS, CAROL!

[*Beat.*]

Charlie saved me, honey. I was—I owed this guy, I didn't
have the money, he put a gun to my head. Right here. Like
this. You know what happens when you're starin' down the
barrel of a gun like that? You know what you think about?
All the shit you never did or said that could've made a
difference—that could've led you down another path. I
was thinkin' about you. About your red dress and Charlie
with his arm around you and how I thought I was lookin' at
my future wife, despite that Charlie is my boy. I was thinkin'
about the time my mom didn't come home that one night
from the crack house and how me and Charlie went to get
'er. I was thinkin' about that, one day I wanna see little kids
runnin' around with my cheeks and your eyes and both of
our stubborn personalities—I saw a million things, in like,
the whisper of a second. Talk about a time machine . . . the
split second between here and dead, that's a time machine
. . . Next thing I knew, ear-splitting shot, and this dude's face
goes slack. He crumples, hits the floor like a puppet when
you cut the strings off. Then I see Charlie, .45 in his hands,
shaking. That's the truth . . . Charlie killed a man, 'cause it was

that guy or me. That's why—the real reason why—I had to help 'im. I had to try to make it right for him too—had to get that body outta there. What can I tell you . . . I fucked up. I always fuck everything up.

BIG SCARY ANIMALS
Matt Lyle

Dramatic
MARCUS, 40–50, African American

After a long, difficult evening where everyone else has shared something true about themselves, MARCUS finally makes his confession.

MARCUS   I hate my brother, too. I hate him. He's . . . Growing up he was always superior to me. He was bigger and stronger and straight. He called me faggot more than he called me Marcus. Then he just failed. Over and over again. Got mixed up with that woman and, yes, drugs. He couldn't stay out of jail. Our parents worked so hard. We were middle class. And he chose that. I hated that. And he got to have a kid. I was doing everything right. I was making a future. I had love and was in graduate school. Making a real career. And he was able to have a kid. One night Clark and I got a call that she was in the ER. When the police went in, they were asleep, and she had pulled the television over on herself, her parents so high in the next room they couldn't be bothered to help that little baby. We took her home from the hospital and she's been ours ever since. How could he not have wanted what turned out to be the most important thing in my life? And she looks like him. Nothing like me. She looks just like him. My . . . one of my aunts, years ago, called me and said that he was clean, had been for years, was working at Wal-Mart, and he wanted to see her. He wanted to be in her life. He'd heard so much and he was so proud. I said fuck no. She is my child. She's mine. Even if he is changed, I couldn't bear to see her with him. Even if it made her happy. Especially if it made her happy.

BOMBER'S MOON

Deborah Yarchun

Dramatic
LLOYD, 28, British

During the Blitz in London in 1940, LLOYD, 28, a working-class East Ender and volunteer air raid warden, speaks to KATRIN, 27, an American socialite he's sheltered with the past three nights in the basement of a music shop. LLOYD has just revealed to KATRIN that he has a wife and daughter sheltering in one of the tubes (London's subway system). KATRIN is horrified by this because LLOYD had previously attempted to seduce her. She's threatening to leave their shelter. LLOYD is revealing himself fully to KATRIN for the first time.

LLOYD   You said you wanted to know me. LOOK. My eyes . . . My eyes is my house in pieces. Windows gone. My front door, lying in shambles. Eyes because you can feel it—y'know, too close to the blast—you can feel your eyes sucked from their sockets. LOOK. My . . . arse is the railway goods yard in Stepney. Tilbury shelter, excrement and margarine on the floors. The crypt we stayed in one night that shuddered. My liver's South Hallsvile school. Where 600 stayed five nights ago. The officials' attempt to evacuate Canning Town. The night an 800 kilo bomb struck the school. And 600 people of Canning Town perished. Just waiting for adequate shelter! LISTEN. My boots. They're the officials not listening. Not listening. NOT listening. I'm A.R.P, but they're not listening! Except a bloke, he's offering to take Tabitha out to the country, God knows where. Fuck. Not in a million years—not after bloody Operation Pied Piper whisked her off for two bloody months. Seven years of age, alone. See my gut; it's where Tabitha's come back from a nice home in the country with bruises. See the space between my gut and heart. It's their weight. Mary, the Cockney girl I married at eighteen, extra heavy in her bridal gown with Tabitha inside her. My veins are the tubes, thousands of people lined in the tubes, crushed against the walls. Tabitha and Mary crushed against my veins. There's a map. See. So, now you know the whole of me. Katrin, a tube was hit. Earlier tonight. 8 pm. While I was on patrol. 1400 Kilos exploded at the cross passage. At Balham tube. That could have been Blackfriars. That could have been Mary and Tabitha. They don't know how many are dead. The tubes aren't safe. There's nowhere safe. There's nowhere safe.

BOMBER'S MOON
Deborah Yarchun

Dramatic
LLOYD, 28, British

*During the Blitz in London in 1940, LLOYD, 28, a working-class
East Ender and volunteer air raid warden, speaks to KATRIN, 27, an
American socialite, in the basement of a music shop. They met the
previous night when they both used the basement as a makeshift
shelter during an air raid. LLOYD has just discovered KATRIN has
returned with a suitcase. He's both concerned about KATRIN's safety
and attracted to her.*

LLOYD   This place might not hold, y'know. That's why I'm here.
I came back. 'Case you were here. To warn you. This place
could collapse. Why do you think the owners abandoned this
place? I snooped around. Left everything. Even the instru-
ments.

[*He puts two and two together.*]

Blimey. You are living here—aren't you? You got somewhere
safe you can be? An ocean liner anywhere else? A place you
can stay in the country perhaps?

[*Re: the basement.*]

Sixty-five percent chance of survival here. Maybe fifty-five.
The science of my arse. But I'm serious. Not even a direct hit's
needed. Any bomb within two hundred feet's likely enough.
There's that bomb beneath St. Paul's still. Undetonated. See?
Wooden rafters. This place's all beams and columns. You see
the ones outside? Two damn near collapse. Ribs cracked.
And all the shrapnel on the roof? Roof's timber. This place
has all the structural integrity of a slum house. And I know
slum houses. Born within the sounds of the bells of Bow, so
they say. May Bow's bells never be past tense. Say that ten

times fast. See those cracks? The wall's starting to bulge? Means the building's moving. Swaying. I officially pronounce this space profoundly unsafe.

[*Through the following, he makes the sounds of bombs. As if counting each casualty with each successive explosion:*]

There goes the Leather Tannery. Atkinson's Perfumery. Sarson's vinegar. Young's Glue factory. Two hundred Stepney souls. Twenty more. All that'll be left when those columns and beams crack are the last bits of structure. All walls and windows. Like a body's spine and neck's broke and it's holding together by its teeth. See. This is the look of a slow progressive collapse.

[*He demonstrates a slow progressive collapse, caving from the top downward with his hands. He demonstrates with his entire body. For a moment, his body is curled, as he holds himself, folding inward.*]

Then the whole building pins you. Holds you tight. The world passes you over. So tight you can't even scream when they come to dig you out. You've nice hair. It's possible the sun might catch it the next day and the rescuers see you. Don't you got somewhere safer to be?

BOTTICELLI VENUS
Don Nigro

Seriocomic
VESPUCCI, 30s

VESPUCCI *is a wealthy man living in Renaissance Florence. He is an ally of the powerful Medici family but secretly hates them and fears that both Medici brothers are after his beautiful young wife,* SIMONETTA. *Here he is telling* BOTTICELLI, *who has been painting* SIMONETTA, *how difficult it is to be married to a beautiful woman who doesn't love you. He is leading up to asking* BOTTICELLI *to spy on her for him, and implicitly threatening him if he doesn't. In fact* BOTTICELLI *is also in love with* SIMONETTA; VESPUCCI *doesn't know that yet, although part of him might suspect it.*

VESPUCCI   You're a lucky man. I thought marriage to this divine creature would make me the happiest man on earth, and I've never been so miserable in my life. What does she want? What does she mean? What is she thinking? What did I do wrong? How can I make her happy? Why won't she do what I tell her to? If you have a dog and you can't train it, you just get another dog. But what am I supposed to do with a woman so beautiful I want her all the time and I can't think about anything else and she treats me like I've got the plague? She's my wife and she won't even let me touch her. She says she has a weak heart, and an infirmity in her lungs, and sometimes she can't breathe, but then I catch her in the back alley with a bunch of little gypsy girls doing cartwheels. What kind of man puts up with that? I'd beat her, but then she might never speak to me again, and if the Medici saw her with a black eye, they might kill me. They both want her. Especially Giuliano. All the women want him, but he's only a little better looking than me, don't you think? He's not as ugly as his brother, of course, but personally I think they're both ugly. All the Medici look like rats. I didn't say that. Don't ever repeat that to anyone. I don't know what I'm saying. I have a shameful secret. My secret is that I am deeply and hopelessly in love with my wife. It's a horrible thing to love one's wife. One should respect one's wife like one's mother but love somebody else. That's the way we Italians have always done it. Even the Pope does that. I don't mean the Pope has a wife. I mean if the Pope loves somebody, it isn't his wife. It's somebody else's wife. Or maybe an altar boy or two. I have no idea what I'm talking about. That girl is driving me insane. All good things are destroyed by love. Listen, the next time you paint her, do this for me: draw her out. Ask her questions. Find out who she loves. Who she's sleeping with. I don't mean to make it an inquisition. Just scatter these questions casually in among the conversation. And then report back to me. Could you do that for me?

BOTTICELLI VENUS

Don Nigro

Dramatic
VESPUCCI, 30s

VESPUCCI *is a wealthy man in Renaissance Florence, married to the much younger* SIMONETTA, *the most beautiful woman in the city. He has stumbled into the studio of the painter* BOTTICELLI *on an Easter Sunday morning, having been drinking all night.* VESPUCCI *has earlier come to* BOTTICELLI, *who has been painting* SIMONET-TA, *to get him to spy on her, as he's convinced she's been unfaithful to him with someone.* VESPUCCI *thinks it's the Medici, but in fact her lover is* BOTTICELLI. *Here he reveals, with a mixture of malice and melancholy pleasure, how he has in fact murdered his wife. He will also reveal later that the Medici are also to be murdered this very morning.*

VESPUCCI   Hey. Botticelli. What are you doing, sitting there in the corner like a horse turd? It's Easter Sunday, and I've been busy worshipping all night at the brothel. Christ is risen and so am I. What's the matter? Do you miss painting my wife? Poor creature. I miss her myself. I don't know why. When I married her, they told me she had a weak heart, but I was so blinded by her beauty, I scarcely heard a word they said. It's a lucky thing she did, though. Now I don't have to sit home and worry about where the hell she is every night. I know where she is. Love is like poison. So, have you seen much of our friend Giuliano de' Medici lately? The fellow who wore her colors at the joust. The one Poliziano writes his stupid poems about? Now, there was a man who loved my wife. Do you want to know a secret, Botticelli? I can tell you, because you're nobody, and because it's Easter, and soon there'll be nobody left to complain to. I learned a secret from Lorenzo de' Medici, who probably learned it from the Pope. It's about how to administer poison. You don't do it all at once. You need to be patient. Just give a little bit at a time, until your victim gets weaker and weaker, as if maybe they had consumption. It was that little Romany girl who told me. I suppose she thought I'd be proud I'd fathered a whelp. The wife, you see, was with child when she died. But here's the joke. Here's what that crazy gypsy didn't know: in all the time we were married, my wife never let me touch her once. Not once. The one time I tried to force her she grabbed the candle and set my ass on fire. I couldn't ride a horse for a month. I can't believe I was actually stupid enough to think she was a virgin. So what was it? A mystical nativity? An immaculate conception? And I was not about to raise Giuliano de' Medici's bastard child for him. Not me. Not with the entire population of Florence whispering behind my back how much the creature's ugly face looked like him. No. I draw the line at that particular humiliation. But here's the thing about poison: it works too slowly. She was very stubborn, my beautiful whore of a wife. She had so much life in her. I just couldn't wait any longer. And she was very weak, by this time. So it was the easiest thing in the world to just put the pillow over her face and press down until she stopped struggling.

BOTTICELLI VENUS
Don Nigro

Seriocomic
FRA LIPPO LIPPI, 50s

FRA LIPPO LIPPI *is a lusty, hard-drinking Renaissance friar who is
also a great painter, the teacher of* BOTTICELLI. *The Medici keep
locking him up so he'll finish the paintings of them he's promised
to do, but he keeps climbing out the window and heading for the
brothel, where he is now with three young women, trying to explain
to his disciple* BOTTICELLI, *who has tracked him down and is trying
to get him back to his studio before the Medici find out, why art is
important and how the artist must be deeply immersed in life.*

FRA LIPPO LIPPI   Art is not a profession. Prostitution is a profession. All right, I suppose art is a profession, but it's also something else, or it isn't any good, no matter how technically
proficient it may be. You can't be a great artist if you spend
all your time inhaling paint fumes. If you don't make a rope
out of your bedclothes, climb out the window and minister
to the nymphs once in a while, you'll always just be a mouse
among rats. It's life that makes art. No life, no art. The Medici
aren't the first or the last rich bastards who think they own
us, just because they have money and we don't. What we've
got, they can't buy, and they know it, and a part of them will
always hate us for it, as much as they might deny it. An artist
is made of flesh and blood. I know about flesh and blood.
I was an orphan in the streets, living on orange rinds the
Medici threw out in the garbage. I let them make me into a
monk so I could eat. But the monks didn't know what to do
with me. I was always scribbling faces all over everything,
drawing naked women and lecherous bishops on the walls,
and penises in the margins of their precious manuscripts.
Well, remember this, Botticelli. Sometimes the best thing
in the book is what's scribbled in the margins. God lives in

the marginalia. And it's a sin to sentence a child of eight to an entire lifetime without the feel of a woman's naked flesh against him under the covers. So I started climbing out the monastery window to go to the brothel, and I've been doing it ever since. We're all beasts. That's our secret, and not a very well kept one, either. The best thing God ever did, among a great many very stupid things he must have made when he was drunk, was to put a woman in the garden. I thank God for that every time I get on my knees to pray. A woman is a creature who means intensely. And the more life one lives, the more one comes to see that everything means intensely. Good or ill, it means. I've spent my life crawling out windows, looking for that meaning, scribbled there in the margins. And so they made a painter of me, and that's where I found God: hiding in the margins, along with food and drink and women and life. That's what God is: a bewildering profusion of realistic detail. Creation is the manifestation of God in us. And why we create is women. We create to understand women, because that's where we feel the presence of the deity most intensely. And we fail. We always fail. The truth is, we're just not smart enough to understand women. But the adventure itself is glorious. You and I and all of us in our doomed and forsaken and noble profession, we are all, in the end, the deformed and broken scribblings in God's margins. And that is our badge of honor. If you want to understand art, look in a woman's eyes. Get lost in her, and you'll find yourself, and your art, and the best in you, and the worst, and everything you need to create until God paints over you. You don't want to be a saint, son. They're all insane. Of course, any artist worth his salt is also insane, but at least we make something out of our madness. And the most glorious madness in the world is to love a woman completely, and with all your heart. That's what makes art. Come on, girls. I'll take you all three on at once. And if it kills me, at least I'll meet my Creator with a smile on my face.

A BRIEF HISTORY OF PENGUINS AND PROMISCUITY
James McLindon

Comic
KING, 35

KING *is serious, angst-ridden, and prone to saying exactly the wrong thing. Nevertheless, he is a good-hearted, immensely likeable sort. Here, he reveals to JULIA, a Harvard professor of linguistics, the secret of an aphrodisiac he has discovered.*

KING   I've studied the penguins' mating patterns for ten years. Godforsaken lonely work, but I welcomed it as a refuge from the cruel rejection by women that has been my lot in the life. In the end, however, the penguins proved immensely satisfying. That sounds bad. I do not speak of the, the love that dare not squawk its name. Rather, after several years, I had discovered that even the ugliest runt of a penguin gets to mate. This fact deeply embittered me, to whom mating had always been denied. For months, I quit my research. But then the scientist in me came to the fore: I had to know the why: why they *all* succeeded where I always failed. It was then that I discovered . . . the penguin aphrodisiac. The male emits a spray that makes him irresistible to the female. No one had ever harvested it to study. I did. I'd . . . rather not say how. Anyway, I'd collected a tremendous amount the year before we met, but it had no noteworthy properties. Not even a discernible smell, even after I concentrated it 1000 times. I naturally assumed it has no effect on humans. But . . . In fact, I discovered it to be the most powerful human female aphrodisiac in the world. Or, strictly speaking . . . *you* did. Seven years ago this very day.

A BRIEF HISTORY OF PENGUINS AND PROMISCUITY
James McLindon

Comic
KING, 35

KING *is serious, angst-ridden, and prone to saying exactly the wrong thing. Nevertheless, he is a good-hearted, immensely likeable sort. Here, he explains to* JULIA, *a Harvard professor of linguistics, a humiliating secret.*

KING   I, I . . . you see, I suffered a, a harvesting accident just before I left last week. I nearly died. I've been harvesting like mad for the last seven years. I plan to sell enough to make me rich and keep enough to make me . . . popular. But harvesting had become increasingly difficult. The penguins don't much care for me anymore. To harvest, I have to get quite close. Last week, as I positioned the collection unit in front of this big cock—[*Embarrassed.*] I mean, of course, a male penguin—He objected with a ferocious nip, knocking me off balance. I slipped, knocked my head on the ice, passed out, and apparently . . . got sprayed.

[*He turns away from JULIA, an anguished, haunted man.*]

Why can't I remember what happened!? When I came to, I was naked as a jay bird, surrounded by several dozen female penguins whom I recognized from my research to be in an advanced state of arousal. More disturbingly, others appeared to be . . . to be . . . to be in what I recognized as . . . a post-arousal state.

BUT WHEN I STARTED TO PLAY!
Max Baker

Seriocomic
FERDINAND, 30

The play is set in the latter half of the twenty-first century, about twenty years after the Tilt. FERDINAND (aka Freddy) is part of a family that lives in a rundown, off-the-grid boarding house far from civilization. Here, FERDINAND is talking to TILLY, a complex, guarded woman from the City who has rented a room in the house for unknown reasons.

FERDINAND   You're one of God's ideas. You deserve all the gifts in the world.

[He digs in his pocket brings out a clear plastic bag folded neatly.]

This is the bag I used to keep my Bible in when it rained. I found it in a community dumpster outside a vacuum cleaner factory when there were still factories. And dumpsters and communities. My theory is it was used for one of the attachments, fabric brush maybe or that nozzle part. That's why I thought it'd be good for my Bible. Turns out the Bible's full of shit You get to the end and there's no punchline It starts out good enough, when God's putting everything together. And then he gets mad and destroys everything and builds it again then tells people to do certain things and if they don't they'll be smited, and some people do what he says and some people don't, which is very exciting. Then he Immaculately impregnates an unmarried Jewish girl. Spiritual Rape, I liked that part. And out pops Jesus telling everyone to go Fuck themselves. Not like, in the way you and I would, more in the "Be Kind To Other People" way.

Which is essentially Fuck You to any asshole making money who turns his back on some poor bastard with no teeth living in a cardboard box. Jesus is kinda my hero. Although he got a bit egotistical thinking of himself as the ultimate human sacrifice to appease the God of Judgment. But rather him than me I guess. So, okay, I'm hooked. The Bible. Great Act One, sensational Act Two then what? Reva-dumb-lations. The most Incomprehensible ending to any book ever written. Samuel Beckett wrote better endings and he didn't even have any storylines. So I threw the whole thing away, buried it in the swamp out back. I thought a tree might grow there. Nothing did. But I kept the bag. The bag meant more to me than what was in it. The only gifts worth giving are the ones you've treasured yourself. I never understood how buying new things and giving them to other people passes for generosity when it all it does is strip the planet dry. I won't take No for an answer.

CAN'T LIVE WITHOUT YOU
Philip Middleton Williams

Seriocomic
DONNY, mid-30s

DONNY *is a best-selling romance novelist who writes under the name Amanda Longington. He is talking to a character in his first novel.*

DONNY   When I got you to Boulder I was also down to my last hundred bucks. I hadn't sold an article in two weeks. The life of a freelancer in New York isn't easy, and the temp jobs were drying up . . . not that I didn't love being a data input specialist for a real estate company anyway. So, I'm scrounging through the aisles of this little *bodega* on Bleecker Street for my weekly supply of Top Ramen when I come across this collection of romance novels with these impossibly syrupy characters written in this appallingly bad style, all written by someone with a name like Heather Golden and Sylvia Frothington. So, I figure, what the hell . . . maybe I can crank out one of these. A week later, I have a hundred pages of this incredibly cloying crap, using every cliché known to man . . . we're talking heaving breasts and husky voices, throbbing manhoods and bulging biceps—the whole nine yards. I used my last stamp to mail it to the publisher just for the hell of it as I'm on my way down to see about getting a job waiting tables at Joe Allen. Three days later I get a phone call. *They want it.* They can't wait to read the rest of it. They say I'm the freshest new voice in romance literature—they actually call it that—in the last twenty years. Two days after that, Barbara Solomon, the literary agent who wouldn't return my phone calls a month before is suddenly trying to take me to lunch at the Russian Tea Room. She's the one who came up with the name "Amanda Longington." And . . . There you have it. Another great literary career is on its way.

CAN'T LIVE WITHOUT YOU
Philip Middleton Williams

Dramatic
BOBBY, early 20s

BOBBY, *a character in a romance novel written by a man under a female name, wants to know why he has not been in any more of the writer's novels.*

BOBBY   It was a Guilt Date. You slept with her, you felt guilty about it, so you tried to treat her like a girlfriend. But you know what she was thinking? She's going, "Look, you're a nice guy and you're good in the sack, but you don't have to feel like you need to take me out as a thank-you card, and besides, I don't expect it. It's not like I'm going to think of you like a boyfriend or anything . . . it was just a nice little recreational romp and let's leave it at that." And that's the way it's been ever since. Am I right? Oh, come on, I'm the last person you can lie to. Face reality. She likes you and you like her. But you two aren't really each other's idea of a match; it just worked out that way. You were roommates, brought to-gether by ad on a bulletin board at a mom-and-pop *bodega* in the Village. You both made enough money to cover the rent and share a fridge, and you didn't get in each other's way. She didn't have a boyfriend, and you didn't either. You liked the same kind of music, neither of you smoked, and you both kept the place reasonably clean. And after a while, you got to like each other . . . you shared some things about work, got to know each other's friends, and people started to think of you two as Donny-and-Anna. And one night, after a nice bottle of white Zinfandel and some Dave Brubeck on the stereo, you're sitting on the couch talking quietly, and just like your best friend's cousin Jack . . . . And when it was over, you were so relieved because you had done jt—you'd proved to yourself that you could do it and like it. So all you had to do was just keep on doing the same thing for as long as you could. You were safe. And that was the last time you thought about me.

CAN'T LIVE WITHOUT YOU
Philip Middleton Williams

Seriocomic
BOBBY, early 20s

BOBBY, *a character in a romance novel, appears and confronts the novelist, who writes under the name Amanda Longington, about what he is doing with his life.*

BOBBY   Who are you? Where did you come from? Where are you going? What great question in life do you answer? What do you symbolize? Four hundred years from now, will you still exist on paper, or on film, or in the minds of great scholars as they review the great fictional characters of literature? Will you achieve the stature of Hamlet or Juliet; Stanley Kowalski or Blanche DuBois, or even Archie Bunker, or the Fonz, or Homer Simpson? No. The only reason you exist is to entertain some lonely accountant sitting in an airport lounge waiting for the shuttle to Boston, or some frustrated matron in a beauty salon whose husband went from being the star of the football team to being the assistant merchandise manager at the lumber yard and is putting it to the blonde bimbo window sales rep when she stays at that neon-clustered motel off the interstate. What happened? When you and I started, it was great. You were going to make me into the next Holden Caulfield. You had such drive, such ambition. You couldn't keep away from the typewriter, writing for hours—getting that crazy Puerto Rican hooker next door pounding on the wall at two o'clock in the morning to get you to stop. And when you finally got that cheap little Apple computer and started all over again, it was like a second chance! But slowly . . . almost like you didn't even mean to, you stopped writing every day. Sometimes it would be for a couple of days. Then you'd go back and change things . . .

first my grandfather died, then he lived . . . by the way, that's very confusing for a character, just so you know. Make up your mind, will ya? And then these romance characters start showing up. They all look the same, they all talk the same, they all are as thin as cardboard, and they're all running around with these dopey names like "Brie" and "Brandi." That's not a novel, it's a catering menu.

THE CHINESE LADY
Lloyd Suh

Dramatic
Atung, 20s–60s, Chinese

It is 1837. A Chinese teenager named AFONG MOY is put on display as a curiosity in a travelling exhibition, and ATUNG is her translator. Here, in direct address, ATUNG tells the audience his dream.

ATUNG   I will tell you a secret. I like to look at the white women. The white women with their white dresses and flowery hats, their parasols and lace. When I look at them in real life, I imagine tearing off those dresses and tossing their hats in the sea, I dream of breaking their parasols into fractions and ripping their lace from their bodies with such wild abandon it causes these women to moan in delight. I also like to look at the white men. The white men with their ridiculous mustaches and too-tall top hats, their booming voices and splotchy skin. When I look at them I dream of biting their flesh to watch as it reddens, I dream of burying my face in the jungle of their woven hair, I dream of overpowering their maddening power with a power they've never imagined, making them submit to my charms until the volume of their voices subside in soft, supple whispers of breath, like a caress. I know what these daydreams mean. I have an appetite for what I cannot have. And because I cannot have anything—In this life, you see . . . I cannot have anything. So it is natural that what I want. Is always that which is *most* forbidden. What is most forbidden to me is not the white women. It is not the white men. The physical act of love that occurs between me and Afong Moy . . . *That* is what is most forbidden. For it comes from a different impulse and a different emotion. It comes from the desire to possess. I know I can never possess a spirit like the spirit of Afong Moy. She is like a wisp, a memory, an idea, a poem. A poem about the sadness one feels after a brief fall of rain, so slight it leaves only a hint of dampness on the earth, and soon the roaming sun will evaporate completely any evidence that such a beautiful rain ever existed. This is not something one can possess. One can only try to enjoy it while it lasts. In order to illustrate this point, you will not see us again for many years. This has been my dream. Or at least, the part of my dream I am willing to tell you.

CHURCH & STATE
Jason Odell Williams

Dramatic
SEN. CHARLES "CHARLIE" WHITMORE, 40s

CHARLIE *is speaking to a crowd of about eight hundred supporters three days before Election Day. (He is up for reelection.) A shooting at the elementary school his two young sons attend took place ten days ago, causing* CHARLIE *(a lifelong Republican and gun rights supporter) to question his stance on the Second Amendment and his faith in God.*

CHARLIE   Now this ain't about taking away guns completely, y'all know I've been a proponent of the 2nd amendment for a long time—heck, I'm a proud gun-owner myself! So you should know I'm not here to take away your rights. I'm here to protect them. Protect the most valuable one of all: Life! For we are all "endowed by our Creator with certain unalienable Rights." But "Liberty and the Pursuit of Happiness" don't mean squat if you're worried about taking a stray bullet to the head while you're out shopping for a toaster! And while I firmly believe in our God-given right to protect ourselves, I don't think our Founding Fathers in their infinite wisdom could have foreseen firearms being sold at a mall right next to that toaster! Because for me, this isn't about "personal liberties." It's about living without fear. And I for one am tired of being afraid. Afraid of the backlash from the people in my own party. Afraid of the NRA and the lobbyists. Afraid for my kids to go to a mall. Or the movies. Or to school.

[*His emotion overwhelms him. He softens.*]

Their own school. And have to wonder if today's the day someone turns a gun on another unsuspecting crowd. So prayer is not the answer. Staying quiet out of respect to the victims isn't the answer. You think those families from Oak Grove, Columbine, Virginia Tech, Tucson, Aurora, Newtown, Charleston, Orlando, Las Vegas, Parkland, Santa Fe, Pittsburgh would rather we sat on our hands another 10 years and let thousands of people die out of respect? No, they want change. And I need you to help make that change. To speak out with your vote. And that, my friends. Just might restore my Faith. In this country. In humanity . . . . In God. Because even though I lost my way, you all have the power to help me find it again! Help me believe in the power of the human spirit to make this country strong! For as the prophet Isaiah says: "Even youths grow tired and weary, and young men stumble and fall; but those who hope in the Lord will renew their strength. They will soar on wings like eagles; they will run and not grow weary, they will walk and not be faint!!"

I'm Charles Whitmore and I sure as hell approve this message.

THE COUPLE NEXT DOOR
Donna Hoke

Dramatic
VANCE, mid-30s

VANCE, *a zookeeper, tells his wife after a week of silence how he felt about the swinging experience they have shared.*

VANCE   We have great sex, we're not afraid to have fun, and I thought we could share this great fantasy and it would bring us closer, like all those things I read online. So we go over there, and all night, there's just this anticipation, this tension . . . It's like I'm back in college, talking up some girl in a bar, not knowing how it's going to end, but hoping—And excitement, adrenaline from knowing we're about to do something forbidden, rebellious. And I have the coolest wife in the world for doing this with me. So when the clothes start coming off, I go with it. It feels like an amped-up strip poker game where we won't just end up naked wondering why we even played. Then Janet starts—Put her mouth on me and I was like, "Holy fuck!" this is really happening. She's going at it, and I'm oblivious to everything else . . . How much wine did we have? . . . And Janet gets me to the brink and she flips over on her stomach and tells me to take her hard from behind. So I do. I put it in, I'm lying on her, and she arches up and her hair is in my face, and . . . And I realize that she doesn't smell like you. And she doesn't make those little noises you make, and her hips don't fit in my . . . hands . . . right, and . . . I want you, Sadie. I don't want to be in this strange woman, I want to be making love to you. Looking in your eyes, feeling you. But my dick has a mind of its own. I start to . . . to come, and I look over, and I see you and Rich, and you're so far away. And fuck, I almost throw up while I'm coming. I never felt anything like that before. Ever.

(DON'T) LOOK AT ME
Molly Goforth

Comic
ART, 60s

ART is a retired self-made millionaire afflicted with just enough non-life-threatening ailments to fuel his pathological hypochondria. His chief hobbies are berating his doctors and relentlessly complaining about his symptoms to his retinue of friends and acquaintances—most of whom maintain relationships with him solely because of his occasional bouts of generosity. ART has an enlarged prostate and a urinary blockage that is being treated with a catheter until he undergoes surgery to remove the blockage. He is not dying. ART suffers from chronic pain due to past spinal trauma, which makes him irritable and short-tempered. He has a portable morphine drip and a private nurse. He is used to being listened to, obeyed, and made much of. Being infirm offends his ego. In this scene he is being visited at home on by his much younger and somewhat dimwitted girlfriend, who has just suggested that he try a chewable aspirin to combat the pain he's experiencing.

ART   I can't take chewable aspirin! I told you! I'm very delicate! I have a delicate system! I can't just take things like that. Last night I took a stool softener and I was giddy for hours, I couldn't even think straight, I took it and then fifty minutes later I felt like, "uhh!" I couldn't even get my thoughts straight. I was on the phone with Margot and finally I had to say, "Margot, I can't even understand what you're saying, I feel like I'm not even in my body, I feel like I'm having and out-of-body experience." And she said, "Oh, my God. What did you take? Did you take something? You can't just take stuff, you're not like normal people." And I said, "I know. I took a stool softener. I know, oh my God, I took it and I'm just like, 'uuuh!' you know when you're just like 'uuuh!'? Oh my God,

I feel so dizzy and lightheaded and just weird." I don't even know what to do, I can barely handle it. I feel like my brain is breaking up into pieces and falling down a drain. I need to put my head between my knees. It was like my brain was breaking up and falling away, like it was falling down a black hole, or a drain and I ended up putting my head between my knees right there on the phone with Margot. I can't take things like that. I can't just take things like stool softeners. It's all I can do to stand being on this morphine drip. It's completely freaking me out, I can barely catch my breath. This piped in air conditioning is driving me guano, I can't even draw a breath. I try to take a breath and it's like "uhh!" I can barely breathe normal air, let alone air conditioning. I can barely breathe normal air!

(DON'T) LOOK AT ME
Molly Goforth

Comic
ART, 60s

ART *is a retired self-made millionaire afflicted with just enough non-life-threatening ailments to fuel his pathological hypochondria. His chief hobbies are berating his doctors and relentlessly complaining about his symptoms to his retinue of friends and acquaintances—most of whom maintain relationships with him solely because of his occasional bouts of generosity. He is used to being listened to, obeyed, and made much of. Being infirm offends his ego. Here,* ART *is in the hospital recovering from prostate surgery. At the top of the speech he is leaving a voicemail message for his much younger girlfriend.* ART *is furious that she did not show up before he went into surgery. In the second half of the speech, he takes his frustration with his girlfriend out on a nurse, although he is also genuinely annoyed about the consistency of the Jell-O.* ART *cares passionately both about food and about being accorded due respect.*

ART   [*On the phone.*] Well, here I am, and where are you? . . . I distinctly remember telling you that they changed my operation to Thursday. But no, you don't want to come and see me in the *hospital*, it's only worth it to you if the old guy's shelling out for medallions of veal at some fancy place where you gotta pay to use the can. I tell you, I worked in an abattoir when I was a boy until I got drafted, and I don't remember a single carcass that had *medallions* on it anywhere. Flank steak was good enough for people once a year on their anniversary, if they could get it. We called it "London Broil" back then. Hold on.

[*to a nurse.*]

This Jell-O sticks to the wall! I'm going to save *this* Jell-O and *dinnertime's* Jell-O and tomorrow *morning's* Jell-O, because in this place apparently Jell-O is a *breakfast food*, and I'm going to put a little *installation* of Jell-O right here on this thing, right where the light will give it nice backlit effect. And then I'm going to stud the Jell-O with some of these hard-on pills and I'm going to call it *Modern Geriatric Medicine, Opus 1* and I'm going to charge your water buffalo rear end $16.00 per viewing every time you waddle in here . . . and then I'm going to put a photo of it on a *tote bag* and make you buy it before I let you out, and *then*, when I get *out* of here, I'm going to send you a letter asking for seventy-five bucks so you can *sponsor* next year's installation where a plumber will caulk a shower with the tapioca pudding that passes for dessert around here, and as you fold up that letter and stick it in your tote bag, you will know that I was right, the goddam Jell-O sticks to the wall!

DEAD MOVEMENT
John Patrick Bray

Seriocomic
RESIDENT, fading 30s-40s

PATRICK *has taken up residence in an historic hotel somewhere hidden in the Hudson Valley. He sits up all night reading newspapers in the small lobby. Another resident enters and talks to* PATRICK, *giving him a sense of what kind of place this really is—a refuge for the lost.*

RESIDENT   Freight comes through at 3:45AM. I've been awake for a half hour. Karie will be getting up soon. She still has a job working as a baker. Kept it through college. She gets to go in just a little later because she has seniority. The early days were tough. And free. We've been clean and sober for twelve years. Six years, because there was a night. Four years, because there was that morning. Three years, because one afternoon someone said. Two years, because it rained. One year, because it didn't. Three months, because I didn't come home. Thirty two days, because I met someone and for a moment got lost in her eyes and I thought she might feel the same way but she didn't, and that was my mistake, but she and her friend drove me home, and my God I owe them, and I hope no one took pictures, and I hope it doesn't appear on social media, I fucking hate social media, but I can pull it together and call it a migraine, a migraine is all it is, my eyes hurt in the same way, and if they don't, I can pretend that they do and wear glasses, and smoke clove cigarettes and be everything you wanted me to be when we were in college and be everything I wanted to be when I hit my thirties when I wrote the great American novel, the text on writing the great American novel, the movie deal for the great American novel with a well-placed cameo that makes folks know I'm the great American novelist, scholar, actor, and personality, and I'll be on Fallon and be hilarious and hang out with Rusted Root and go to parties with Snoop Dogg and it's 1993 and everyone is still alive and still high and still looking forward to the future which promised no baldness no beer guts just endless chiseled good looks that come from honest places in America, summers of eating strawberries and peaches and knowing no matter what happens next we'd be safe because we've always been safe and to take that away would be a lie.

DOWNTOWN RACE RIOT
Seth Zvi Rosenfeld

Dramatic
TOMMY-SICK, 18, Italian American

TOMMY-SICK *is a wannabe gangster. He is speaking to his good
friend* P-NUT, *18. He is disarming* P-NUT *with this story before
hitting him with the news that* P-NUT *has got to help set up his best
friend's murder.*

TOMMY-SICK   Check it right, so everybody's high, they got like
tunes playin', I'm tryin' to get laid, no dice. All the chicks leave
and Jay's over there making out with Cassie so I'm like fuck this
I'm gettin' the fuck outta here, right? But Jay's like cool out for
a minute, right. So next thing I know he's bangin' Cassie right
in front of me and truth be told I start catchin' a woody just
watchin' it, right? But in my mind I'm kinda like this is fuckin'
perverted watchin' this kid have sex. And he's goin' all out but
not cumming. For like twenty minutes straight, Marone! So
now she wants to get handcuffed. My hand to God, this kid
has handcuffs on him. He handcuffs her and he's like take your
turn. To me! I'm lookin' at her, ya know, cause I ain't no fuckin'
rapo and I'm goin' is this okay? She's like, "you're cute, I like
your eyebrows." This chick likes my eyebrows! So you know I'm
nervous but what the fuck I'm not gonna panic at the pussy.
That ain't me. I take off my clothes whip out the swanson-john-
son and it was so sweet, Nut. Reallyreally sweet. I didn't want it
to end. Finally Jay's like "cmon bro, it's four in the morning." So I
get up and she's like can you uncuff me now? Jay's like No. I'm
like Jay uncuff the girl. He's like fuck her let her stay that way.
I'm like have a fuckin' heart. The chick is starting to cry and I'm
like Jay! He says to me this is the game they play. He leaves her
cuffed up all the time. Her parents find her they punish her and
the minute she's off punishment she calls Jay and they do the
whole thing again. [*Pause.*] Can I get a beer?

THE DRAMA DEPARTMENT
James Hindman

Dramatic
ROB CHALMERS, 30s to 50s

ROB *is a very enthusiastic drama and debate teacher at Chippewa Valley High School. He is sociable, charismatic, out for the good of the student. He is speaking to* DAVID*, a new sophomore at Chippewa.* ROB *cast* DAVID *in the lead role of the fall musical but, after being bullied by the head of the school board's son,* DAVID *wants to back out.*

ROB   David, wait . . . Look, I get it. I get why you're nervous. Greg Barns and his friends are only picking on you because you're the star. And I know how intimidating that can be . . . but you can't quit because of a bunch of bullies. David . . . when I was in the ninth grade . . . I had to be the shyest kid in school. Painfully shy. And I had this teacher. Mr. Alderson. Meanest old grump in the world—and one day . . . he thought he was going to fix me. He made me get up in front of the class to write the Gettysburg Address on the board. I shook so badly I couldn't even lift my arm. The chalk melted in my hand from perspiration. Finally he told me to sit down. Cut to two years later. Mrs. Williamson's English class. She loved the theatre. So passionate. So inspiring. She asked each of us to learn a Shakespeare monologue . . . and one day she said, "Who wants to perform for the class?" To this day, I have no idea how I got there but the next thing I knew . . . "Speak the speech I pray you as I pronounced it to you, trippingly on the tongue; but if you mouth it as many of your players do, I had as lief the town-crier spoke my lines." And all that pain . . . all that fear . . . vanished. "To be or not to be." "To dream the impossible dream." It all matters. That's what I want for you, David. Please don't quit. Don't let them win.

EDUCATION

Brian Dykstra

Dramatic
MICK, 17, biracial

MICK *is a high school senior who is in trouble for making an art project in which a flag would be burned. He was stopped before the burning and the principal is giving* MICK *a chance to defend his choice of burning the flag. This is* MICK *listing some of his reasons while he's trying to get out of being suspended from school.*

MICK You guys. Adults. Your generation. Or were you just going to claim you got handed this mess? I mean, were you guys asleep? And then we slap up a flag and wave it in their faces, chanting our patriotic theme song, USA! USA! Which, I don't know, might just be the exact opposite of the intelligent response. There was a artist did a piece called September 12, 2002, one year after 9/11. He went around on that day and took pictures of a bunch of the flags that had been so proudly displayed. They were totally forgotten. Left to rot. Yeah, that's respect. "But oh, no, an athlete is kneeling during the National Anthem! Oh, My God! Let's all panic! That guy never gets another job!" And how does the flag represent everything *except* the freedom to protest? Or should I say the *Liberty* to protest? *Oh, no, it's disrespectful to the troop*s—and, yeah, we get it, the troops, the troops, the troops, but it's not about the troops! It's not even about the flag! It's about inequality. And Black Lives Matter! When did the flag become exclusively about the troops? You want to support the troops? Figure out a way to help them not be one of the 22 every single day who commit suicide! What does it even represent; Land of the Free? Please. We have 5% of the world's population and 25% of the world's prisoners. And most of them look like us. Or darker. What? What did I just say? Is that even possible? 25%? Hey, maybe THAT'S why the quarterback is kneeling, ever think of that!?! And mostly because drug laws are stupid. And prisons are a business! Anti-drug campaigns packed full of total lies in order to keep weed from competing with their line of "mood enhancers." And let's not kid ourselves, their drugs side effects suck. Way worse than weed. No one bothers telling the truth. It's just total scare tactics, trading on stereotypes that anybody who's smoked a single bowl knows is total bullshit. So, why should we believe you about other drugs? You lied about weed, you did every drug imaginable growing up and it didn't kill most of you, half you all are addicted to booze and pills to help you sleep (Oops, opioid epidemic. Just like every other drug dealer) way too many of my friends were medi-cated with Ritalin or whatever made raising them easier on their lazy parents. And rather than diet and/or exercise we take this pill for cholesterol and that pill for blood pressure while eating mayonnaise on everything, including bat-ter-dipped fried cheese. Fuck are we eating? Ya' know?

ENTERPRISE
Brian Parks

Comic
OWENS, any age

OWENS *is a businessman. He is at the end of long overnight effort to come up with a plan to save the failing corporation he works for. Frazzled and stressed, he is addressing a colleague he's been working with on the plan, angry at the company's staff.*

OWENS   Where's the rest of the overhead projector?!

[*In a building rant.*]

We need it for our presentation. Goddamn this place! Who let this happen? *Who?!* Bureaucrats, that's who. Slack nine-to-fivers. I'll kill 'em, I will! Why is this office so full of them? The second rate, the C-plussers, the semi-wits! And they all work on *our* support staff. Support? *Support*?! We support *them*! We bring in the cash so they can sit all day refining their incompetence, anuses digging deeper and deeper into their seat cushions. The meek will not inherit the Earth, oh no. The half-asses will! The world is nothing but half-asses. The continents half-assed, the countries half-assed. It's half-assed people in half-assed towns with half-assed pets and half-assed country clubs with half-assed members backwashing their hepatitis into gin-and-tonics. They go to half-assed churches with half-assed heavens, heavens full of half-assed angels looking down on all the half-asses doing their half-assed screwing, the vigorous copulation of the mediocre, over and over, parts slapping and splatting, thurping and squirting, making little zygotes—little half-assed zygotes that pop out, shake off placenta, and rule us all!!!

EVANSTON SALT COSTS CLIMBING
Will Arbery

Seriocomic
PETER, 30s–40s

PETER *is in a truck, salting the roads, talking to his partner,* BASIL.
He has something of an obsession with death.

PETER   Oh everyone's saying Nutella can cause cancer. You haven't heard this? It's in all the tweets. And all the articles about the tweets. It's cuz of the palm oil. Cuz apparently palm oil, when you heat it up, it's cancer. And there's a ton of palm oil in Nutella. But who knew that? They didn't know it caused cancer. How could they know that? It's not anything Ferrero did wrong. Ferrero's the company that makes Nutella. I know that cuz my brother-in-law works there. But now all the stores are all pulling Nutella off all the shelves. Yeah it's crazy when I saw the news, I was like, "my brother-in-law works for Ferrero." He sells Nutella to Wal-Mart. He goes down to Arkansas and sells Nutella directly to the Wal-Mart family. They're scared. My brother-in-law. And his friends at the office. The office in New Jersey. They're just people. They see the news on the internet. They drive to work the next day. They're all like: "Oh no—look at this news story. It's about us." "Fuck. I'm gonna kill myself." "Hey, good morning everyone." "Oh hey Gary." "Did you hear the news?" "Yeah we did Gary. Fuck." "I'm so sorry, Gary." "Me too, Francine." "I'm gonna kill myself." "Yeah, just do it, just kill yourself." "No, don't. We'll get through this somehow." "Yeah. Don't worry." "We're all in this together." "I love you." "Fuck don't say you love me." "Why?" "Cuz it hurts, it hurts to love you, it hurts to love all you people." "Fuck." Fuck. One little tweet and suddenly Nutella means cancer. You start to understand why oil companies and, you know, gun people, plastic people, pharmacy people and whatever, fight back. Why they try to stay on top. Cuz they're just people. And they all want to kill themselves. Because the world doesn't need us. Not one little bit. It would be better for the world if we all killed ourselves. The planet would thank us. And we all know it.

EVERYONE'S FINE WITH VIRGINIA WOOLF
Kate Scelsa

Comic
NICK, early 30s

NICK SLOANE *is a professor in this outrageous parody of Edward Albee's classic play.* NICK *has come to* GEORGE *and* MARTHA's *apartment with his wife,* HONEY, *in the hopes of charming his hosts into helping him get a tenured position at the college where he and* GEORGE *both teach. When* MARTHA *answers the door,* HONEY *awkwardly blurts out that she has just found out that she is not pregnant. In order to try to save the moment and to change the subject to one of his favorite topics,* NICK *explains to* MARTHA *and* GEORGE *that he loves to write mpreg, a subgenre of fan fiction in which the author takes some liberties with preexiting fictional characters, in this case, Jacob and Emmett from the Twilight series.*

NICK   I was pregnant once, but only in fiction. I used to write
    fan-fiction, and then I moved on to slash-fiction, which is fan
    fiction where you make everyone gay even if they're not.
    I believe I mentioned this earlier at the party? Well! Then
    there's this thing called mpreg where you write about pre-
    existing fictional male characters having sex with each other
    and then getting pregnant. For example a werewolf and a
    vampire from a popular vampire-centric franchise; maybe
    their names are Jacob and Emmett? I don't know, it's just an
    example. But I was spending a lot of time writing stories for
    the slash-fiction community message board, and it was also
    this thing called Mary Sue where one of the characters is a
    thinly veiled version of yourself, and you're really just writing
    it for your own pleasure, as your own secret kind of fantasy
    that maybe you should have kept to yourself. And this is re-
    ally looked down on in the community because it's not seen
    as generous. And the slash-fan fiction community is really

into generosity for some reason. Like you're all sharing this secret sexuality of fictional gayness. So the point is that I was writing slash mpreg, but the pregnant character was a Mary Sue version of me, so it was like I was pregnant.

THE EX-GIRLFRIEND EXPERIENCE
Rhea MacCallum

Seriocomic
ROBBIE, 20s and up

ROBBIE *addresses the woman he has hired to portray his ex-girl-friend for a date night and instructs her on how to best capture the essence of his ex.*

ROBBIE   Angela's a copyeditor for the local newspaper. Small circulation. She tells everyone she's a writer working on a novel, but . . . she was working on that same novel since before we met. Never did see her actually, you know, writing though. [*Pause.*] Anyway, none of that really matters because what I want you to keep in mind is that she was very critical. About everything. That's what I need to you capture in your portrayal of her. Be mean to me. As mean as you can possibly be because she could be intentionally cruel. Criticize my hair-cut, my clothes, my cooking, wine choice, the awkward way I laugh when I'm being scrutinized, anything really. And smirk a little when you're insulting me, sometimes. Yeah. That would be a very Angela thing to do. Be relentless. If you think something might cross the line and go too far that is exactly the thing I want you to say to me. There was no "too far" with Angela. Know that. I know we haven't . . . had relations . . . but mock my stamina, length, girth, everything. Emasculate me. I mean it. I'm sure you're normally a lovely person and maybe this isn't the kind of service you're used to providing. I'm sorry if it makes you uncomfortable but I guess you took this assignment with some kind of understanding of what you were getting yourself into, so yeah, that's what I need from you. Abject distain. Belittle me. Bring me to the verge of tears or anger. Frustrate me with my inability to please you. Kill me with your cruelty. Got it?

A FISH STORY
Richard Manley

Comic
WALDO, 20s–40s

WALDO, *a dramaturg, is having his first meeting with a reluctant playwright,* DAVID, *who is coming out of the business world and starting very late in life.*

WALDO   Look David, I don't give a shit about you missing your IPO or getting sued by your CEO for breeching your NDA or any other acronymic bullshit. I'm not here to make you feel safe. You're scared and you should be . . . you're starting very late, have no credentials, and nobody's ever heard of you, but there's a very good play in here, waiting to be finished, and I believe there's a very good playwright in there, aching to begin. Of course, you'll be overwhelmed by rejection at first, probably start drinking, then turn to heroin, you'll blow through your savings, and end up at stage doors, begging for scraps of food, and after losing all dignity, you'll have an epiphany and realize you can return to the ad business, where you'll once again make a good living writing crap.

[*Handing him a piece of paper.*]

While you're finishing the fucking play, here's a reading list of books on craft, support organizations to join, theaters an' contests to which you should submit work. Revisions first, then I'll charge you . . . a lot. Your watch cost more than my car. Sooner or later, you'll realize how foolish this business really is . . . the way romance is foolish, or hope, or the joy that can come from a single memory, and then you'll really wonder what the hell you're doing. But people still weep when Nora gives her final speech, and when Willy dies, and when Blanche is taken away, and they long for more. Now beat it, I have work to do.

FLOWERS IN THE DESERT
Donna Hoke

Dramatic
JOE, 41

JOE *defends his parenting to his ex, who he thinks is telling him he's not doing enough.*

JOE   And you know how you know I'm not doing enough? Because you've got me on a fucking reward chart. You've got Matt's and Zane's hanging there on the refrigerator, and mine is right there next to them. It may as well be. It's in your head. Only instead of getting points off for not putting the toilet seat down, I get docked if you find a mac and cheese box in the garbage or if I let them watch too much TV. And if I help with homework or take them to the library—gold star! You don't get to dismiss me. If I don't know every little detail about them, it's because you kicked me out and you don't tell me. But I've driven them to the emergency room, and cleaned up the puke when you were gagging too much to do it yourself, and I got in that second grade bully's face last year, didn't I? Like it or not, I am their father, and you can't measure how much I love them by my score on some . . . trivia quiz. What the hell do you want from me? Is it gonna take a freaking contract? Signed in blood that I will never disappoint you. That you can kick me out if I don't what? Teach them one new vocabulary word each day? Is that the healing you need? What about me? Surprise, Britt. I'm still just a regular guy. I like burgers and baseball and beer, and at the end of a long day at the cube farm, I like to have dinner with my family, maybe throw the ball around with my sons, watch some TV, and fall asleep next to the woman I love. Because I do love you, and I love those kids, and fuck you if you don't like the way I do it.

FREE PASS
Tom Baum

Dramatic
WAYLON, 60s

WAYLON *has struck up a conversation in a hotel bar with* TARA, *a woman he has mistaken for a prostitute. On the verge of early onset Alzheimer's,* WAYLON'*s wife gave him a "free pass" to have one-time sex outside the marriage. Intending to cash in on this offer,* WAYLON *finds himself pouring his heart out to* TARA.

WAYLON   OK . . . how can I put this . . . my wife and I hadn't been intimate for some time. I mean I could still function, otherwise I wouldn't be wasting your time. And so here's the thing. Before she . . . before Sally became seriously ill . . . while she was still . . . when she had all her faculties . . . She said she would understand . . . if it was temporary . . . a one-time thing. See . . . my wife . . . some years ago . . . earlier than most people . . . Sally lost touch . . . with the person she used to be. That's when we stopped being . . . intimate. She . . . well, basically, she turned into a child. Happens to folks every day, all over the world, but when it happens to you . . . when you've stopped having relations . . . with the person you love . . . that you loved the first time you laid eyes on her . . . You kinda forget what the fuss was all about. She knew I . . . she knew I'd never do it on my own. If there's one thing I'm sure of, Sally and I were faithful to each other. From day one. Or-phans of the teenage storm, that was Sally and me. See this jacket I'm wearing? These socks, this shirt, these slacks? She bought them for me. Everything in my closet, down to the laces on my shoes. I'd head for the changing room, she'd toss things over the door. She had very good taste. We'd have clients in for dinner, she set a beautiful table. All my buddies were crazy about her. They told me as much . . . afterwards

. . . when it was safe . . . safe to say things like that . . . . I used to lie in bed at night . . . and if I couldn't hear her breathing, I'd reach over in the dark and touch her . . . as softly as I could . . . just to see if she'd stir . . . and then . . . one night . . . nothing . . . no response. I turned on the light and there she was. Eyes wide open. I shook her and shook her. Nothing. She was gone. I couldn't stand living in our house anymore, I had to sell it, sell everything, every stick of furniture, every knickknack, I couldn't bear to look at anything. I considered moving to another state. One where assisted suicide is legal. I felt so damn guilty. Towards the end, you don't know what it's like, she was angry with me all the time. Tantrums every night. I pictured what life was going to be without her, and I liked what I saw. Sally, she didn't want to end her life, any more than a three-year-old child wants to die. The truth? Every time I think about it now I want to kill myself.

FUCK MARRY KILL

James Presson

Dramatic
BRANDON, early to mid-20s

BRANDON *is an amiable burnout who has chosen to stay home
and take care of his dying mother. He has recently summoned his
younger brother (who had been off exploring the American West) to
take over familial responsibilities so he can elope with his girlfriend,
Kayla. Smoking weed in his backyard late at night, BRANDON holds
court and explains his reasoning. He is speaking to his best friend,
his now-returned brother, and his brother's friend.*

BRANDON I need a fresh start . . . I've been here my whole
   life, and everything I look at . . . It all has so much baggage
   attached to it. There's so much sadness in the place you
   grow up. Memories are all . . . Aren't they? Aren't they *all*
   sad? Even the happy ones are sad in a way. Cuz life is sad. I
   hate the trees I climbed in and all the sandboxes and soccer fields I played in. I hate my elementary school and my
   middle school and my high school and my shitty fucking
   community college. I hate my mom and Kayla's mom and
   I hate the street I live on and the street she lives on. I hate
   the stone wall in her backyard that I fell off of the first time
   her dad caught us kissing. And all this hate . . . It's just built
   up and built up and now my heart is full of it. My lungs are
   black with it. I just think that maybe I could, like, find myself
   in the desert. Or that Kayla could. Or maybe both of us could.
   But even just one would be fine. If one of us did, we could
   help the other one. You know what I mean? We'll have all the
   tools. We'll have a little house made of mud or something.
   Adobe. We'll have a grill and I'll have my truck and we can
   drive through canyons and shit. I want the sand, y'know?
   And the red rock and the crazy fucking sunsets. I want the

cactuses and the lizards and the dust in my face and the work gloves, all of it. I want to live like pioneers. Like on the Oregon Trail. I think we can do it out there. We'll go to Vegas, but we'll only spend one night. And we'll get married. And then we'll go to New Mexico. We'll sleep in the sun. Our skin will turn brown. We'll make stuff with the earth, pottery and shit. Our arms will be so strong. And we won't even fuck, y'know? We'll just make love. I've never done that I don't think. There are so many things I haven't done . . . Fuck this place, man. Fuck the grades and the judgment and the picket fences and the block parties and the delis. Fuck all that shit. Fuck Mondays, Tuesdays, and especially fuck Wednesdays. Fuck church and school and practice and assemblies and carnivals and pancake breakfasts and youth group and auto shows. Just fuck everything. I hate every single speck of it. Yo, check it: in the desert we'll make tacos all the time. We'll only drink wine with fruits in it. It'll be so *refreshing*.

GREEN WHALES

Lia Romeo

Dramatic
IAN, 40

IAN is speaking to KAREN, *who's a woman in her thirties but who he believes to be a teenage girl.*

IAN   Okay. Well—let me start at the beginning. Up until a year ago, I was married. She . . . was cheating on me. With one of her coworkers. She was with him for three years and never told me. All the "work" dinners, drinks with "friends," "business" trips . . . I finally got a call from his wife, which was how I knew my marriage was over. I met my wife when we were young—both sixteen—and once I met her I honestly never looked at anyone else. But then after the divorce— well, on my way home from work there's a high school. And I'd drive by it and see the girls' soccer teams practicing, and . . . one day I stopped and watched them for a while. It wasn't . . . a sexual thing—I don't know—it was confusing. They reminded me of her, when she was young, when we first met. And it made me feel better to watch them. And then I met you. And it makes me feel better to be with you—to talk to you—I feel like I've been frozen, and every time I see you another little piece of me thaws. First my feet, and then my calves, and then my knees. That's, uh— that's as far as I've gotten. I've gone out with a few women since my wife and I split up, and none of them have made me feel like you do. I don't know . . . I feel like I can trust you. Maybe it's because you're young—but you just seem so . . . . Whenever I go out with a woman my own age, I can't help feeling like she's lying to me somehow. And of course she probably *is*—about how old she is, or the color of her hair, or how much she likes baseball— because that's what people do when they've first met. But I can't take it. After what happened with my wife, I just—can't take it. I don't want to be with a woman who's lying to me about anything.

GUNS, GOD AND GOMORRAH
Joseph P. Krawczyk

Seriocomic
VIRGIL, early to mid-40s

VIRGIL *is trying to convince JOEL, a former combat veteran who has killed sixteen innocent civilians, to embark on a journey with him to a metaphorical place, which he has to conquer in order to redeem himself for his crimes.*

VIRGIL   When the hell are you going? I'm your guide, remember, me, Virgil. Get that through your thick skull. You can't go there by yourself. You need me and all the help you can get. You think you're the only one who has gone to Gomorrah? Not many have come back unscathed. You're not the first, not by a long shot, and you won't be the last. It's a place where Caligula dwells in his spare time. A place so obscene that certain serial killers have vacationed there on humid summer nights. It's a heaving, haunting terror where crazy-eyed vintners have gone to till the sunless, windless soil that no impressionist would dare to paint because only a surrealist would feel at home there. The place is a juxtaposition of the familiar and the unfamiliar, taxing the mind to become convoluted into a pretzel-like chamber of horrors that demean what humanity you have left. It's a gross misrepresentation of real life. It's like a moonscape without a moon. Nothing like anything I've seen before. And it's quiet, no breeze, everything's as still as a battlefield littered with dead bodies. Not even the smell of death. just a paralysis of movement and time. It makes you wonder if you're still alive. All feeling deadened, because it's a haze . . . everything . . . just a haze . . . Before, you were the gung-ho king of the jungle, cutting a wide swath through the vines. But that feeling fades fast when your nerves become numb. When your eyes exhibit that blank stare of indifference. When your brain is anesthetized to all forms of pain and suffering. And you walk like a man without a heart because it has been sucked from your body and deposited into a black hole. You can't deny that, Joel, can you? And that's the trick, isn't it? Keeping your thoughts in symmetrical order before they devour and consume your outer layers so that you're no longer recognizable even to yourself. Joel, we haven't got time to dawdle while you dick around the maypole tree. Don't be an ass. Procrastination will only prolong the agony. So, let's go, let's move out. You want to be whole again, a more perfect, although flawed, human being. Don't you want that for yourself?

HARMONY PARK

Daniel Damiano

Dramatic
ERNIE, mid- to late 50s, African American

Months after a racially charged argument served to end the friend-
ship between ERNIE, *a landscaping foreman, and* MIKE, *a younger*
white landscaper on his crew, MIKE *returns to attend the ribbon*
cutting ceremony for the park in the hopes of patching things up.
After a bit of awkward small talk from the two prideful men, ERNIE
eventually opens up about a pivotal point from his past.

ERNIE   I never told you much about my wife, did I? Yeah, well
. . . She was . . . She really got me in a way I didn't think any
woman could. Smart, sweet, didn't take my shit, didn't suffer
fools . . . And one funny-ass woman, too. I mean, she'd make
me piss myself sometimes, that's how damn funny she
could be . . . Anyway, 7 years into us bein' married, she got
sick. Fuckin' liver cancer. 32 years old. [*Pause.*] She needed
a transplant, 'n' she was in line for one. But bein' in line for a
liver is like bein' in line for a bar a' gold, y'know? It ain't like
the kidneys, where everyone's got one t' spare. So we waited
for someone t'die so she could live, until she couldn't keep
livin' herself anymore. [*Pause.*] Somehow I found out that
the liver that shoulda' gone t' her ended up goin' to some
alcoholic sitcom actor. White dude. [*Pause.*] I found that out
. . . 'n' it seemed like as soon as all the tears had left my ducts,
they were replaced by my hatred a' every white sitcom actor
I ever saw. [*Pause.*] Then every white actor. [*Pause.*] Then
every white *man*. [*Pause.*] I was one bitter sonofabitch for a
long time, Mike. Roberta was gone. Was never gonna have
the family we wanted . . . 'n' all I had was myself t'look at 'n' it
got t' where I was even hatin' that. So eventually I jus' started
t' ease out a' that way a' thinkin'. Started to realize the energy

I was expendin' on bein' so angry. So I stopped drinkin' too much, eatin' too much, even took up yoga, started writin' . . . Got my shit together 'n' jus' . . . began feelin' like life was here for me instead a tryin' to fuck with me, y'know? [*Pause.*] But these feelings can come'n go like the breeze on any given day. And when they go, . . . all the namastes in the world can't much help. [*Pause.*] I guess we're all meant t' be tested in one way or another, or else we probably ain't alive.

HOCKING MURRAY
George Sapio

Comic
SIMON, 35 or older

SIMON, *a diamond dealer, is talking to* DOROTHY, *a middle-aged widow who wants to pawn a diamond ring that, through a commercial process, used to be her late husband, Murray.*

SIMON   Would you buy someone's dead husband? Think about it. You're looking for a quality gem to give as a present, an anniversary, maybe an engagement ring. But the jeweler tells you, this is not just your normal run-of- the-mill diamond. Because of the wonders of modern technology this diamond did not start out as a rock. It used to be a person. That's right, a person. A living, breathing person. It used to be, let's say, Murray. Or Walter. Or Martha. Now imagine this. Once you tell someone that the gem they are looking at used to be a living human being, who will want to buy that? Imagine the thoughts going through their mind. About having Murray or Eugene or Deborah on their finger. How? Because there are those people who have had their loved ones cremated and processed into—technically—real diamonds for sentimental reasons. That, I suppose, is one thing. It's personal. It's familiar. It's a balm to a stricken, broken soul. But everyone dies. And the Murray or Eugene or Debra that graced Barbara or Kareem's finger is now up for auction. So it's not a Murray or Eugene or Debra that you knew, but someone else's Eugene or Debra. A stranger. I know people who won't wear used clothes because they were once on someone else's body. And who knows who this ring may have been? Were they good people? You wouldn't want a murderer or a congressman on your finger. You wonder: Were they attractive? Sane? Tall? Short? Caucasian, Asian,

African-American? Who was this ring you are thinking about putting on your finger? Could you actually wear a diamond on your finger every day and not wonder who it used to be? You see, diamonds are meant to be admired, to be looked at, to be revered. But they have always been intrinsically without identity. But this. Knowing it was someone named Murray or Eugene or Debra, how could you stop looking at it, wondering who Murray was? And what if you did the research? What if you could discover the provenance? So you look this ring up and find a picture. What if Kareem now has a face, a full name, an identity? To know that the ring on your finger used to be an actual human being with skin, organs, a brain. A scent. A penis. You look at the ring and now all you see is Murray. How would you feel about wearing a once human on your finger? But let's retract a bit. Let's say the ring is actually someone you knew and loved. Someone you laid next to every night for thirty years. Someone you cooked for, cared for, had sex with. Grew accustomed to as time welded you two together little by little. Could you ask someone else to wear him now? Once you leave him here, what would you do? Could you wear someone else's Martin? Howard? This is your husband. Why, after all this time, and all that expense to keep him, would you want to get rid of him? Worse: to sell him to a complete stranger?

IF I FORGET

Steven Levenson

Dramatic
MICHAEL, 45

MICHAEL, *a secular Jew, has just published a book that argues that the obsession with the Holocaust by American Jews has turned them into a culture obsessed with death. He thinks that Jews should stop making everything about the Holocaust. His sister SHARON disagrees.*

MICHAEL   And there it is. Thank you, Sharon, for demonstrating the entire thesis of my book. The best way to win an argument about Israel? Change the subject back to the Holocaust. The Holocaust has been used, the idea of the Holocaust, to distort American Jewish life, and discourse, and culture, since the 1960s. Until today, now, it's now, I mean, go into any synagogue in America, the Holocaust is now the centerpiece of Jewish life. The lynchpin that binds us together is suddenly, it's not culture anymore or food or religion— it's certainly not religion, with the number of American Jews that actually practice their religion—it's the six million. And we've been manipulated, all of us, our entire lives, to feel constantly victimized, constantly afraid. You hear it all the time: "It could happen again, never forget, because it could happen again." It already has happened again. It happened in Bosnia, it happened in Rwanda. It just didn't happen to *us*. We learned all the wrong lessons from the Holocaust. We learned that the world hates Jews, that the world will always hate Jews, instead of what we should have actually learned—that nationalism is a sickness and it is lethal. And the book argues that the only way we can escape what has essentially become, at this point, a religion and a culture of frankly death and death worship, a culture that finds its meaning and its reason for being in the charnel houses of Europe, the only way we can get past that is if we forget it. Actively. We stop making movies about it and writing books about it, celebrating it, venerating it like it's this, like it's, it's—because otherwise, if we don't, I feel, I argue, at length, in the book— if we don't forget the Holocaust, now, if we don't begin to disentangle ourselves from our own obsessional neurosis, then we'll be, that's the end of us, this will be our last chapter. As a people. If we can even call ourselves that anymore, when the only thing that connects us to one another, that connects us to ourselves even, are ghosts.

[*Silence.*]

I don't believe in ghosts.

IF I FORGET

Steven Levenson

Dramatic
LOU, 75

LOU *is the patriarch of an American Jewish family. His son* MI-
CHAEL, *a college professor, has just published a book that criticizes
Jews for being obsessed with the Holocaust. This is* LOU'*s response.*

LOU   At Dachau, I don't know if you came across this in your research or not, but when the Americans liberated the camps
at Dachau—you have to remember, they didn't know what
we know now. They didn't have a word for what they were
about to see, to walk into. They thought it was a POW camp.
Every door they opened, every room, the floor to the ceiling, they found bodies stacked up, one on top of the other.
You can imagine the smell. Coming from everything. From
the gas chambers. From the bricks of the crematorium. The
ovens. From the dirt under your feet even. On your boots.
The ones we found, the ones who were still alive . . . it was
the worst with them, the smell. Coming from off their skin,
their breath. And they were so hungry, Michael. The GIs gave
them food, rations. Some of them, they were so hungry, they
ate it so quickly, no one could get them to slow down. And
so their stomachs ruptured. After all those years and they
ended up dead of a full stomach. But some of them, they
weren't hungry. They didn't want to eat. They went back
and they found the guards, the Germans, and they rounded
them up. They took shovels, they found shovels and bricks
and sickles, and they hit them with the shovels, with the
bricks, and the sickles. The Germans who had killed their parents or maybe their brother or their children, right in front of
them. The Germans with full stomachs, uniforms starched.
They took the shovels, men who didn't weigh a hundred

pounds, you could see the bones sticking out of their skin, they took the shovels and they smashed their faces in over and over again. On and on. Some of the Americans even . . . they helped. They herded them together, the guards, and they gave their guns to the prisoners and the prisoners shot them one by one. Like animals. Like Jews. And the Americans, they just watched. We just, we stood and we watched. And we were glad. My God. We were glad. I'm still glad. [*Pause.*] For you, history is an abstraction. But for us, the ones who survived this century, this long, long century . . . there are no abstractions anymore.

ISMENE
David Eliet

Dramatic
CREON, 50–60

The play takes place on year after the death of ANTIGONE *and* CREON's son, Haemon. *Locked in his palace together because of their fears of the Theban elders,* CREON *because he caused Antione's death, and* ISMENE *because she would not share her sister's fate.* CREON *is speaking to* ISMENE. *He is mocking her need for meaning in life after all they have been through.*

CREON   Do you know why man invents things—out of bore-dom. All of his inventions grow out the tedium of existence. He grows tired of tilling his fields with a stick. "I know," he says, "that big animal over there, the one I call 'ox,' if I could just get him to pull the stick, my job would go so much faster, be ever so much easier." So he tames the ox, and he invents ropes to tie the stick to the ox. Only the stick keeps breaking, and he gets bored with having to find and fashion more sticks, so he says to himself, "I need something stron-ger. I know, I'll sharpen that stone and attach it to the wood." But sharpening stones in turn becomes a dreary task, so he discovers how to melt ore, and pour it in a mold to make an even better plow. And if he can melt stone to make plows, he can also make spears, and swords, and candlesticks. And soon there are men who do nothing but mine the ore, and others who make it into all those wonderful things. And each of them, out of boredom with their tasks, which in them-selves have become repetitively dull, invents new ways to do those tasks better. But sad to say, no matter how much he invents, no matter how much he seeks to find new ways to make his work less tedious, man can never escape the mind numbing routines of his daily struggle to survive, to put food on his table and clothes on his back. And so finally he is forced to ask himself, "why?" "Why must I do this? Just to survive? What is survival? For what purpose do I bother to survive? Why don't I just stop? Because if you do," he says to himself, "you'll die? And what is death? Why should I fear it so much? And what does it matter if I die now or later, since I'm going to die anyway?" And to answer all of these questions, he invents philosophy, and art, and government, and history and religion, just so he can find a reason to go on surviving. And that's what it means to live life, Ismene. That's what it means to live life.

JERRY HOFNAGLE'S TOP TEN LIST
Laura Emack

Seriocomic
JERRY, 44

JERRY *opens up to his comatose father,* FRANK.

JERRY   Dad, I wrote this on the Red Eye while Sarah slept. It's
my top ten list. It's the top ten unspeakable truths I will
say to my comatose father, secure in the knowledge—or
perhaps the mistaken belief—that he cannot hear them.
But what else is new? You never did listen to anybody else's
opinion. Not to me, not to your students, maybe you listed
to Mom. I don't know. I can't remember back to a time when
things weren't broken. Certainly you wouldn't listen to Aunt
Mae when she tried . . . But I'm getting ahead of myself. Here
we go. Number ten: My marriage sucks for the very reason
you predicted. Sarah's eight years on me are etched in her
face. You told me it would happen. Number nine: In 1965 Di-
ane wore the same sweater and plaid skirt to school for five
days in a row just to see if you'd notice. The teachers noticed.
Even the oblivious older brother figured it out by Thursday.
But the distinguished Professor Hofnagle? Number eight.
Chemistry can't explain what's up with Joel. That *Scientific
American* article you sent—the one about aging eggs and
autistic-spectrum disorders? Fuck you! For the very last time
Joel is not a speck on some spectrum. He's got an oddness
that's uniquely his. Number seven. I cheated on my SAT's. I
paid Aaron Burger fifty bucks to take the test for me. Not the
first time, mind you, when I got in the high four hundreds
and you were furious, the second time when I jumped two
hundred points on verbal and scored seven twenty in math.
Number six. Remember when you accused Earnest Miller of
breaking in and trashing our cabin at Oglebay? You got him

arrested and it cost his mom a fortune to keep him out of jail. Well, I smashed the chairs and the mirrors. All by myself. It was after I lost in the final round of the debate tournament and you insulted me in front of the whole world. Mom would have blamed the judges for caving to sentiment. She'd have assured me that, in the universe of truth, I won. Cause I was good that day, way better than the competition. Just because the other kid was stuck in a wheelchair doesn't mean he needed victory more. I deserved my win. Mine.

God! It was twenty-five years ago. Why can't I let go?

JONAH

Len Jenkin

Seriocomic
JONAH, could be any age

JONAH has promised God that if he escapes from the belly of Levi-athan he will preach His Holy Word. God has sent him to straighten out the evil people of Nineveh.

JONAH   People of Nineveh! I know how hard it is sometimes to live in peace with your neighbors. I know how hard it is some days to feed those children who depend on you. I know how hard it is to find a little warmth in this world. How hard it is to find even a splinter of happiness. How hard it is to love God. This is not an all-night party. This is not a circus or a TV show. I am not an entertainer. This is a rescue mission. I am not gonna ask you to leave if you're a drunk, or a drug addict, or if you smoke dope. I am not gonna ask you to leave if you're a whore, or a thief. I'm not gonna ask you to leave if you're running from whatever law they got here, or from yourself. I will never turn anyone away. You ever hear of the children of God? His precious babies. You wonder who they could be? Every one of you. And if you're God's child, and he feeds you, and clothes you, and puts a roof over your head, and gets you born in the U.S.A, and gives you the gift of being able to open your eyes and see the beautiful colors of the sky, what are you supposed to do in return? Steal bread from your mother's table? Gorilla old ladies in the parking lot at the QuikStop? Make a living on your back at the Traveler's Inn? Abuse children? Rape? Kill? Generally fuck up? Hear the word of the Lord. I will burn your chariots in the smoke, and my sword shall devour your young lions. The gates of the rivers shall be broken, and the Palace drowned. Faceless men with machine guns will kill anything that moves, even the dogs.

Burning trashheaps, saltpits, desolation. The cormorant and the bittern lodge in the broken windows, their shrill cries pierce the night. Jackals roam the courtyards and feed on corpses. Ashes in the wind. Nineveh, that great city, will be laid waste, and no one will remain to mourn her passing.

JQA

Aaron Posner

Seriocomic
HENRY CLAY, 51

Senator HENRY CLAY *tells President* JOHN QUINCY ADAMS *that his presidency is doomed unless he learns a skill he has always resisted—compromise.*

CLAY So here's an idea you'll hate. I'm going to use The "C" Word. That's right: COMPROMISE! It's time to compromise, Mr. President, or trust me, you're never gonna get one damn thing accomplished, not in this fractured, fractious America. Open your damn eyes . . . sir! Believe me, it'd tickle my testicles no end if this country was just ONE THING and we could all agree on the right course of action and then just, you know . . . Get Stuff Done! That would be just peachy . . . but hell, Johnnie boy, way before this was even a country it was already a vast, steaming shitheap of impossible contradictions and irreconcilable incongruities. You've got your pure-ass puritans . . . and your pretentious scientific/enlightenment fancy-pantses stirring up no end of trouble with all their *knowledge* and *facts* and . . . holier-than-thou-*rightness*. You've got your wildly *religious* and even more wildly *irreligious*, goin' at it like cats and . . . *cats*. You've got frontiersmen heading out west to settle the wilds, and wild folks heading to the cities to make them cesspools of chaos and confusion. You've got your stuffy old English and your fancified French and those God-damn clock-work Germans and Austrians and Swiss, for God's sake . . . and a rung or two down, you got your Irish and Italians and A-rabs and Chinese and Mexicans and God knows who-all just pouring in from every point of the compass. And Jews! You can't forget the Jews just . . . Jewin' it up all over the place . . . Oh, yeah, and then there are all those pesky rust-colored folks who were here when we got here who just won't seem to painlessly disappear just because we want them to . . . and these other folks who we've been *importing* in droves since we arrived to do all the work, and who now, by God, insist on being treated like human beings themselves, and where the hell that'll end up God only knows, but it won't be simple or easy or a helluva lotta fun, you can bet on that! Right, missy? My God, you are the President of more than ten million souls right this minute, and hell, I don't know about yours, but my own damn family can't agree on which book to read aloud after supper in less than an hour of squabbling, and that usually includes more than a few tears shed and a few voices raised, and that's over a thing of no moment and no consequence within the same damn family! Nope. No easy solutions. No "getting along." No unanimity and consensus. Nosirree-Bob. Not in these here "United" ha ha ha "States of America." Not never! Yet folks keep on bellyachin' and wishin' we could all just "get along" and "want the same thing," which would be excellent except for the fact that it will never, ever, EVER happen! And I'm not so convinced it would be a good thing if it did . . . ! Disagreement keeps us sharp! Keeps us on our damn toes! Trust me: You'll need to learn to COMPROMISE if you hope to have an ice cube's chance in hell of getting anything actually DONE during your damn Presidency.

JQA

Aaron Posner

Seriocomic
ANDREW JACKSON, 52

ANDREW JACKSON *has just been elected the next president, making* JOHN QUINCY ADAMS *a one-term president. He has very different views than* ADAMS *about what the government should and shouldn't do.*

JACKSON   You think The Government is the cure for every ill, don't you? You look at the citizens of this country and you think "these little people are so . . . weak-willed . . . so small minded . . . so inherently incapable of caring for their uneducated, unsophisticated little selves that what they so desperately NEED is us Harvard-educated, Greek-speaking, four-eyed Eggheads to figure things out for them and Tell Them How To Live Their Damn Lives!" Build them new roads! Dig them canals! Take away their hard-earned slaves! Force them off their family farms and into public schools whether they want to be there or not! Take away their guns! Force them to pay taxes to subsidize pointy-headed "celestial scientists" to sit in literal towers and stare at the stars so that we can . . . what? Count them? Figure out how the fuck they twinkle? Who the hell gives a flying fuck about the STARS!?! Not real working Americans! How the hell is that going to put food on their tables and keep them safe from Indians and wolves and hurricanes and famine and drought and Real-Life Problems?!? *The Government* is not the country, John. *The People* are the country. The government is here to shoot our enemies, keep order in our streets, and see that the rule of law is maintained. Maybe every now and then declare a holiday or feed a foreign head of state. That's all! That's IT! Even your fucking father knew that you smug, superior son of a bitch! You really want the government to pay for *science experiments* and *art* and *roads* and *schools for every boy and girl*? What next? What the hell do you imagine??? You think the government should supply doctors for every sick person, food for every hungry person, tiny little townhomes for every wayward wanderer??? The most despotic, power-hungry monarch never imagined such . . . intrusion in the lives of their people. The People don't need you! The *best* government is the *least* government!

THE KISTIAKOWSKY AFFAIR
Alan Brody

Dramatic
GEORGE KISTIAKOWSKY, early 50s

It is 1957. KISTIAKOWSKY, a professor of chemistry at Harvard, has learned that there is a secret admissions policy, with a quota on how many Jews can be admitted. He is hoping to organize opposition to this policy.

KISTIAKOWSKY   I'm speaking for the faculty of the Department of Chemistry and for a few others from different faculties. I hope there will be a lot more of you after what I have to tell you. We asked Dean Bundy for this meeting because we have recently discovered something alarming about which we need to inform everyone. Harvard University has an undergraduate admissions policy that includes a quota for Jewish applicants. When I first found out and began to research this I asked Dean Bundy and Dean Bender about it and both said I would not find such a policy written down anywhere. And that was true. But if you go back to the 1930's, you will find that the very reason we began the admissions interview system was in response to a problem of undergraduate Jewish admissions. Before that the only thing the admissions office looked at were test scores. Grades and, of course, whether the candidate was the son of an alumnus. But it turned out that the percentages of Jewish students in the incoming classes were rising and that wasn't because they were sons of alumni. But we couldn't address this Jewish problem directly. That would be discrimination. So we decided to add the personal interview system in order to determine if the candidate fit new requirements. Like "character" and "sociability" and "sense of fair play." Those kinds of things were written down in instructions to the interviewers who were alumni from all around the country. There also seemed to be a lot of concern about how an applicant would "fit in." I suppose you see where this is going. After the interview became a part of the process the percentage of Jews dropped back to a safe fifteen percent. And it's remained there ever since. Harvard has a great responsibility to keep our moral compass true. We cannot, after World War Two, continue this policy of discrimination based on stereotype, prejudice and what is clearly becoming more and more anti-scientific and anti-intellectual. I and Professor Molton, Pappenheim, Williams, Brinton, and Stouffer want to bring a petition to President Pusey demanding that Harvard end the policy of the Jewish quota. Find any one of us after this meeting and tell us if you'll join us by signing the petition.

THE KISTIAKOWSKY AFFAIR
Alan Brody

Dramatic
WILBUR BENDER, early 40s

It is 1957. BENDER, *dean of admissions at Harvard, disputes* KIS-TIAKOWSKY's *charge that there is a secret, unwritten quota of how many Jews may be admitted.*

BENDER   There is no Jewish quota. And I defy anyone here to prove there is. There is no prejudice. There is no discrimination. There have been plenty of Jewish undergraduates in every class I've seen in my years as Dean of Admissions under President Conant and President Pusey. And those students have done well for the most part and we were as proud to have them identified as Harvard gentlemen as any of the others. What's important here is what it means to be a Harvard gentleman, what it is that makes him special. And that's not just test scores and numbers. We are shaping America's leaders of tomorrow. When they leave here they understand the responsibilities of power, whether they earn it through hard work or inherit it. Those aren't things you learn from taking tests and reading books and arguing uselessly about Henry James or Dostoevsky; and you don't learn it from a steady diet of science, either, which is what Professor Kistiakowsky has been trying to force down Harvard's throat even before I became Dean of Admissions. He seems to think the leaders of tomorrow will need to know the arcane ins and outs of physics and mathematics in order to serve the country as businessmen, legislators, doctors, lawyers and that seems to me to be just a little bit self-serving. If it were up to him we would let everyone in who has done nothing but study all his life whether or not that's made him a neurotic, obsessive, or even a la-de-da pansy. We can let the University of Chicago give the country all the eggheads it wants to. That's not our job. Our job is to uphold the traditions of Harvard that have served this country since 1636. If we make the changes Professor Kistiakowsky's calling for we'll be overrun with Jews, Italians, Irish, and then what? Chinese? Colored? Women? How about Communists? How American would that be, Professor Kistiakowsky?

THE LONG REUNION
Jack Gilhooley

Dramatic
BILLY, 82
(Although Billy is 82 at this point in the play, this monologue would work for an actor of any age.)

JIMMY, BILLY, *and* DAISY *are celebrating their sixty-fifth high school reunion at the same seaside restaurant as previously. Thus they are eighty-two years old, since this is the fifth scene (of five) presented in ten-year intervals starting with the trio's twenty-fifth get together at age forty-two.* BILLY *was the Golden Boy in high school, excelling at athletics and academics. But rather than accept a scholarship at a football factor, he chose to attend an Ivy League college. Upon graduation, he returned to his hometown to teach and coach at a quality prep school. This choice was anathema to ex-classmates like* JIMMY, *even now that they are—all three—well into retirement.*

BILLY   HEATHER IS NOT AT BURLINGTON MANOR!!! Heather's in a sanitarium. . . . She had a breakdown twelve years ago. She has not recovered. Never will. She grew bored living in the same place all her life. More than bored . . . she grew hyper . . . unhinged. Before she crashed we had some hazardous times. She'd say that I was so promising in our youth. That's why she fell in love with me. Big football star. Prom king. Major college scholarship. To her, I offered a life of glamor . . . adventure. A way out of here. An exciting future. But it never happened. She always regretted turning down that New York modeling contract. After college, I came back here to be with her. She said that we should've gone forward. We were young and she said that she married me for love. I never asked her what she wanted. I just wanted to stay where I was secure. Safe. And where I'd proven myself. Now she lives in a fantasy world where she's the star model on the international runway. I suppose that I read too much. I thought that love was enough. Cynthia's taking me to see her. Heather hardly knows who I am. But I know who she is.

THE LONG REUNION
Jack Gilhooley

Dramatic
JIMMY, 52

JIMMY, BILLY, and DAISY are celebrating their thirty-fifth high school reunion at a seaside restaurant. Thus they are fifty-two years of age, since this is the second scene (of five) that are presented in ten-year intervals into the future as the tides rise. JIMMY is the flashy and seemingly successful one of the trio. He has become a world-class rock manager since he transformed Sheila and the Nosepickers—a garage band from their high school—into a major international pop music attraction anchored by the beautiful Sheila. He loved ill-fated Sheila since youth, but his devotion was unreciprocated.

JIMMY   It started out innocently enough. A little grass before they went on. Just like back in school. A little booze. It helped, especially the guys. They'd sound almost tolerable. But that's what the boys were all about . . . dissonance . . . chaos. But Sheila was a pure talent. That voice was like crystal . . . delicate . . . perfection. The audience was in awe. The clatter would stop and she'd open her mouth and she'd mesmerize thousands from her very first note. And no one was more spellbound than me. But it's brutal on the road. And fame is a vicious trap. I could go through the litany . . . Hendricks . . . Joplin . . . Cobain . . . Winehouse . . . on and on. For ninety minutes every night Sheila was in total command. But the rest of the time there were the paparazzi . . . the fans out of control. And yes, the boredom. I mean whattaya do all day in Akron? They had to come down every night after a mega-energy performance. The drugs escalated. Coke . . . heroin . . . speedballs. And when we'd tour Europe . . . Amsterdam . . . Copenhagen—my God, there's a whole drug commune in Copenhagen—I was with them in those days. I did my damndest to keep her straight. But it was impossible. I had my hands full with the crazy fans. You read about the guy in Germany who broke into her hotel room. A stalker . . . a complete stranger. I heard her scream. I had a key to her room and I managed to restrain the crazy bastard. I had him arrested. He was out in 48 hours. The cops hate druggies over there. I hadda get a gun. Easier said than done in Europe. Not like here. After rehab, a changed woman. She swore off drugs. Got addicted to Bikram Yoga which was a good habit. She'd sweat all that bad shit out. She dumped her second husband. Deadbeat Number Two. She was looking great again. Then I hadda come home for my divorce. I was more than ready for that. I figured I'd have an open path to Sheila. But when I caught up to them in Belgium, she was using again. Broke my heart.

MAYOR OF THE 85TH FLOOR
Alex Goldberg

Dramatic
DETROIT, late 20s–30s, African American

DETROIT *is a black-market delivery guy in New York City in a dystopian future when all bridges and tunnels have been destroyed, isolating the city. He lives outside of the Empire State Building and wants to be with* ROME, *who hasn't left the building in years.* ROME *has just asked* DETROIT *to describe the route he will take to his next delivery.*

DETROIT   Okay. Leave the building at the main entrance checkpoint. Take a right on Fifth Avenue. Past the gun emporium on 31st. Past Koreatown checkpoint and the labor market. Then the burned out buildings. No need to scavenge, they all empty shells. 23rd Street and the pie slice building. The dead zone. Lots of junkies, but a couple of pills always trade for safe passage. There is this beautiful colored glass on the second floor of a building on 21st. I bet when the sun used to shine, on the inside it looked like a rainbow. Then the dock checkpoint at 17th. I remember when I could walk as far south as 11th Street, but now you'd be waist deep in that dirty water by 13th Street. Before the air was smoggy I could see the old submerged buildings that are still standing in The Village, and the big ones that are still standing past that. What's left of the Freedom Tower in the distance. I don't know how far those underwater blocks go. But now that the last bridge is down, everything is gonna get tougher. Prices for everything is gonna skyrocket, and some stuff won't be available at all. It's already bad. Last week when I picked up a load of booze on the Ninth Avenue docks I was ambushed. I had a knife, but there was four of them with knives. Man, if guns were still legal? Pop pop pop pop. Shit.

MAYOR OF THE 85TH FLOOR
Alex Goldberg

Dramatic
SAN DIEGO, early to mid-20s

SAN DIEGO *is a soldier and loyalist to the Empire State Building,
which, in this near future, has been overrun by a squatter community with its own security force. He has a strong sense of what is
right and wrong, at least according to him. Here, he is telling his
love interest,* ROME, *about his interview for a better position. He is a
lifelong resident of the building and has never been above the 35th
floor until this interview, which takes place on the 60th floor.*

SAN DIEGO   So yesterday I went. I've never seen anything like
   it. It was totally clean. No dirt at all. Windows in place, and
   closed. It wasn't humid or nothing, totally comfortable. No
   wind. Quiet. Behind a big desk this woman was like "may
   I help you" and I told her my name and she was like "we
   were expecting you. Have a seat." They had leather couches.
   Magazines. There were no other people there. So I waited.
   Five minutes. Ten minutes. Who knows? It was so peaceful
   there, it made me nervous. One time there was a ring, and
   the woman behind the desk picked up this huge phone and
   started talking. And get this . . . the phone had a cord attached to it and was connected to a box on her desk! I have
   never seen anything like that. It looked stupid. Anyways, she
   talked on the phone and then hung up and told me to follow
   her down a hall into a room. Small room. Big table. One chair.
   On the table, a pen and a form. She told me to fill it out. It
   was weird. The questions were strange. What did I eat for
   breakfast? When is the last time I used violence? How much
   sleep do I usually get? Who do I love the most? I answered
   myself. And the strangest question, can you fly? I've never
   tried. I wrote down yes, just to be safe. Then I finished and sat

there for, like, ever, but no one came by. There was a mirror on the wall. Floor to ceiling. So I just sit there. 20 minutes. 30 minutes. Who knows? Then the woman from the front came and said I could go. I asked her what's next, and she said "if it's good news, you'll get another envelope."

MEET ME AT THE GATES, MARCUS JAMES
Donna Hoke

Dramatic
MARCUS JAMES, 18

MARCUS JAMES *is finishing his high school valedictory speech, following a hate beating.*

MARCUS JAMES   Mr. S says you have to choose when to make your stand: I choose now. I'm headed to Stanford in the fall— hold your applause—which is kinda funny, 'cause it sounds like "stand for," and I'm takin' that as a sign, because I know that even if you tell me I'm safe, even with laws against hate, or laws that say I can get married, I'm not safe. Not when twenty percent of hate crimes in this country are because of somebody's sexual preference and another fifty percent are because of race. I'm kinda screwed, huh? So my stand starts here and it ain't gonna stop. It isn't enough to say "I would never." You gotta make a Stanford like Matt, and like Aaron, for Jesus, or somebody you love, or how about to do what's right? Because nobody's safe until everybody's safe. When I get to the gates of Heaven, I'd rather be the hated than the hater. We all have that choice. So this is me making my stand. I almost died tryin', and I still might, but I'll tell you this: if I do, and by some miracle, a hater finds a way to meet me at the gates, I'll walk 'em through.

MIC

Brenton Lengel

Comic
BEN, 40s

BEN, *a painter, is discussing the gentrification of New York's Lower East Side with his friend JOSH, a musician.*

BEN   You know what? I blame Rent. I mean the musical Rent. Man, this is the East Village; this is supposed to be Mecca for hippies, burnouts, beatnicks and punks. Then some guy writes a Broadway musical about how glorious it is to be young, poor, artistic . . . positively riddled with AIDS . . . Guy writes a musical and suddenly every young professional, banker, and trust fund kid up and moves here. Hordes of idiots flock to our neighborhood, rent goes up and off we go—victims of the fetishization of our own lifestyle. You ever feel like joining a horde? I do. Every day. But they won't let me in . . . though I do take comfort that if things keep going the way they're going, that horde is going to have to actually join us in the gutter. I wonder if after pretending to be poor for so long, they'll enjoy actually being poor. And who knows? Things keep going the way they're going, maybe everything will collapse and we can move back here . . . And if we're real lucky, maybe we'll get a renaissance. Because that's what you do when the chips are down. Institutions everywhere are crumbling, and the world as we know it is pretty much coming to an end. What a time to be an artist . . .

MOM, DAD AND A BAD IDEA
Sam Bobrick and Joey Bobrick

Seriocomic
KEN, late 50s

KEN *explains to his wife why, even though they are fairly content with their marriage, it's their God-given duty to seek more from life.*

KEN Elaine, sit here for a minute. When I got up this evening, I did some research on my computer. Do you know what the odds are of being born? Do you know what an incredible process it is? Let me enlighten you. I'll make it as simple as I can. Okay, to begin with, a woman is born with about five million tiny little eggs with the sole purpose of reproduction. Imagine five million eggs just floating inside her for years and years, willy-nilly. Nowhere to go. Not much to do. Kind of boring, don't you think? Take my word for it, it is. Okay, now at some point during each month, one of those eggs gets a little bit fed up with doing nothing and makes a break for it through this dark, scary tunnel. Okay, now as that egg starts to travel toward the woman's muffin. I'm more at ease calling it a muffin because it sounds more welcoming and frankly I don't understand them that much. Now if that woman is having sex during the time that egg is traveling down her "whatever," and if the man she's having sex with happily has an orgasm, the man releases millions and millions of tiny little sperm. So okay. We now have six hundred million tiny, little sperm swimming around with only one thing in mind. Finding that woman's escaped egg and fertilizing the hell out of it. But out of those six hundred million sperm, only one guy hits jackpot. Elaine, you and I are the products of that one lucky sperm and that one lucky egg. Against the shittiest odds in the world, you and I won the miracle of life. And to treat it as no more than a given, run-of-the-mill everyday occurrence without getting everything we can out of it, is just plain criminal. We owe it, not just to ourselves, but even more to those two courageous heroes who dared to risk it all so that you and I could have an opportunity to walk in the sunlight. The sperm and the egg! For their sake and for our sake, before it ends, we've got to go out there and seek more. We have no choice. We have to split up. It's our God-given duty.

MOM, DAD AND A BAD IDEA
Sam Bobrick and Joey Bobrick

Comic
KEN, late 50s

KEN HABER, *who with his wife's blessing has decided to seek more out of life, tells his wife and two grown children about his first date since embarking on this adventure.*

KEN   Ahh, yes. Chicago. At first Bunny seemed very disappointed in me. But once I gave her the three hundred dollars she asked me for, everything seemed to go well. She wasn't a hooker. She was a school teacher just supplementing her income. They pay those poor teachers nothing nowadays. Then we went to a dance club. The secret is to bring a girl wearing hip high boots and a bikini. She suffers from hot flashes. Well, Bunny saw I looked a little uncomfortable and for two hundred dollars sold me a couple of pills that she said would change my life which is exactly what we wanted to do, right, Elaine? Luckily, she accepted credit cards. So, I took the pills. In a matter of minutes the entire universe opened up. There were lights, there were stars, there was Elvis. Not the skinny Elvis but the fat, sweaty one from Vegas. He was eating a fried peanut butter and banana sandwich. Suddenly he yanked me on stage with him and we did two numbers together. Don't ask me how we did it, but we sang them in Swedish. The crowd went wild. Suddenly they all raised their hands up high and started screaming at me "Jump Ken jump!" Jump Ken jump!" So I jumped. Right into the crowd. The next thing I knew I was on a human conveyor belt. I got conveyed from the dance floor, past the bar, through the front door and dumped into the middle of the street where a cab driver picked me up and for only a hundred and seventy-five dollars brought me home. Elaine, it's a tough world out there. Now, if someone will point me to the bedroom, the Walrus and I are going to sleep.

MONKEY IN THE SHADE

Steven Haworth

Dramatic
MONKEY, 50s

MONKEY *works at a Louisiana oil field as a derrick man. He is speaking to a teenaged boy named* SEAN *who was kicked out of his home and who has just been hired at the oil field. Here,* MONKEY *explains to* SEAN *who Lucy—a name he sometimes calls out when sleeping between shifts on the oil rig—is.*

MONKEY   Four years ago I'm drivin' a tractor trailer 'bout four in the mornin'. On this little two-lane state highway in the flatlands, Nebraska. I'm poppin' bennies to stay awake. Thinkin' about my family back in Pennsylvania. How my wife is ready to kick me out 'cause I'm never home and drivin' a truck is all I know. I see somethin' down the road. Somebody way down the highway dressed in white, standin' in the road. I think a hitchhiker but then I get closer and it's my sister, Lucy. Standin' in the road. It's the middle a nowhere. Nebraska cornfields for days. She's wearin' her nighty. Barefoot. Her feet all muddy. She's yellin' somethin'. But standin' still. I hit the brakes but I'm going pretty fast. I'm almost on top a her. I see her eyes black as outer space. Still yellin'. I turn the wheel . . . . Jackknife. Wake up in the hospital with two cops lookin' down at me and doctors and all sorts a beepin' an' shit. They tell me three things. First, I fucked up that truck big time, they found the speed in my blood. I ain't never drivin' no truck again. Plus, my wife was notified a what happened. She washes her hands, last straw. Files for divorce. Then they asked what made me jackknife. I told 'em. I saw my sister. In the road. My sister Lucy. Who has the cancer. They're all quiet now. Say we called your wife about the accident she says tell him Lucy died at four o'clock. The room got . . . even more quiet . . . *embarrassed*. Cops lookin' at their shoes. I get out the hospital, wander around. Heard about work down here. I ain't been back to Pennsylvania. Don't happen every day somebody dead drops by on their way out. I saw somethin' of the other side. I saw my sister who I loved like nothin' else on this earth. The mornin' she died I saw . . . a miracle . . . and it completely fucked me up! Took everything. My family. My job. Fucked me up entirely. Tell me why my sister would do that to me? Why'd she do that? What did I do? What did I not do?

MOON MAN WALK
James Ijames

Dramatic
SPENCER, late 20s

SPENCER *has come home after the sudden death of his mother, who he believes to be his sole relative. Going through her belongings he discovers that his father is a prisoner in a correctional facility near where he grew up.* SPENCER's *mother, attempting to protect her child, told the young* SPENCER *that his father was stranded on the moon. Here,* SPENCER *is talking to* PETRUSHKA, *a strange woman he meets on the airplane ride home, about what he knows about the moon.*

SPENCER   Billions of years ago . . . when the earth was just a baby planet, another smaller planet collided with the earth. Just smashed right into it. And it vaporized the earth. Just turned it into a big mass of hot hot gas. I imagine the molten mass being pulled back together from the pull of gravity. Cooling itself and making itself again after the fall out. The detritus of the collision mending and healing. This broken orb looking for its balance and orbit. From the debris . . . a smaller orb formed. It was so close to earth at first. Dancing with her. Spinning so closely that it could almost kiss the lips of the boiling seas. Over time the two orbs learned to live further and further apart but still drawing and pulling on the other in this celestial cha cha. Slow. Slow. Quickquick. Slow. The moon is a part of earth and we are all moon men. Looking for home. Slow. Slow. Quick. Quick. Slow. They still dance. Sometimes they kiss and push us all into darkness. The Moon. That's the story I want to believe. That's what I remember. That's what I believe in.

THE MULBERRY BUSH
James Colgan

Dramatic
PAUL, 50s

PAUL *is speaking to* WENDY, *late 30s, who is his ex-girlfriend.* WEN-DY *and* PAUL *are madly in love, but* WENDY *has commitment issues and keeps breaking up with* PAUL *only to come back a week later and beg for forgiveness and reconciliation, which is driving* PAUL *nuts. After they break up "for good,"* PAUL *moves away. Two years later, he comes back for a visit and he and* WENDY *have supper together, after which they get into a tiff about their breakup.*

PAUL   Look, let me say this and that'll be it, okay? That letter I wrote you, I *was* drunk and I was *really* pissed off—and, yes, hurt, *really* hurt—but I meant every word of that letter. I meant it. I tore up all your pictures and threw them in the dumpster so I wouldn't be tempted to dig them out of the waste basket and tape them back together. I deleted all your text messages and your emails, and I deleted your number from my phone and your email address from my computer and all the pictures of us on my desktop, and I was *never ever* going to even *think* about you again . . . But it didn't work. I couldn't stop thinking about you. And I was a mess. And I *still* can't stop thinking about you, and I'm *still* a mess. About a month before I left, I went down to LA to pitch the novel to a publisher, spent the whole afternoon with the editorial committee, got back to my hotel room that evening and I couldn't remember a damn thing I'd said, because all I could think of the whole time was you . . . And I know you don't want to hear it, but I *still* love you. And I don't think that's ever gonna change . . . So. Again, thanks for meeting me, it's been a nice evening, it's great to see you, but now I'm gonna go, so take care of yourself, have a good life, goodbye.

THE NEST

Theresa Rebeck

Dramatic
NED, 20s–30s

NED is in a bar, on a date. He is obsessed with the imminent risk of pandemics that will kill millions of people. Needless to say, this doesn't go over well with his date.

NED What worries me, what really worries me is not what man does to man. What WORRIES me is what tiny tiny organisms do. To man. Organisms that have no consciousness, or need or desire, organisms that barely exist themselves. But which can can can sweep over the planet, just like like air. Literally! And they can cause such utter, and it's happened, historically, I mean, I didn't even tell you about the bubonic plague, what a holy mess that was in the middle ages, just like once a year it would sweep through Europe and take out a quarter of the population. The rats carried it. But the others, yellow fever and influenza and and cholera, small pox, that stuff is just in the air we breathe. And it's coming again, you know just historically there is no way to stop it, that's why people get so nervous when there's just a moment like SARS? Or the bird flu? All those monkeys, in Washington. Not to mention the very near miss we just got through. The reason those moments are so terrifying is that people know what could happen, in the world we live in now, the air we breathe touches the air that EVERYONE breathes, and people, borders are so porous now. The planet is smaller. The disease that is in one place reaches another so quickly. And the next pandemic, it will kill billions. BILLIONS. And we're not set up to handle something like that and that'll be it. All men will die.

THE NEST

Theresa Rebeck

Dramatic
PATRICK, 20s–30s

PATRICK *is in a bar that has seen better days, owned by his friends* NICK *and* LILA. LILA *has gone back into the kitchen.* PATRICK *thinks it's time to sell.* LILA *is very much resistant to this. She thinks they can fix it up.*

PATRICK   The way she sees it isn't making sense anymore. It doesn't matter how long it's been, sometimes things are around so long that they don't make any sense, and we don't live in a world where that's allowed. History is just too expensive! I mean this place is gorgeous. Anyone can see that. But it's past its prime. Anyone can see that too. You come here, you have a few drinks and a few laughs, it's great. But in the morning the joint doesn't look so hot. Neither do any of us. Listen, we've all had things happen to us here, events, conversations, disasters, good things too, you met Lila here and fell in love, there's no denying that important things happened here. But in another way, another way to look at it is, they didn't happen here at all. They didn't happen in this place. They happened inside you. But this place is evaporating. It's evaporating. Because there's no money. And that's all America is now. They build a TGIFridays a mile down the road, we know places like that are for shit but no one cares. They're loud, they're noisy, the drinks suck but they got commercials on the television and they're in the middle of a mall where it's all money and food courts and multiplexes and you can't even, the light is so bad in those places. The food. It's like all anyone eats is, you can't eat it, that stuff, you can't eat it. Phony cheese dip that someone sticks in a microwave and then they pour it on a tostito. It's worse than Velveeta, that stuff. Who thought they could make cheese worse than Velveeta? I don't know. I don't know.

NYC 523

Joseph Gallo

Dramatic
ALLEN, early 30s

ALLEN *is a tour guide speaking to a group of tourists on the Lower East Side of Manhattan.*

ALLEN   The Lower East Side. Once the gateway to America. And for generations of Jews, Germans, Italians, Eastern Europeans, Russians, Greeks, Chinese, and Latinos . . . it represented the future. An urban frontier where artists, Bohemians, and radicals helped to shape world culture. But idealism, creativity, and the struggling masses of the newly arrived, have recently been replaced by money, greed, and the value of real estate. The Lower East Side as we know it has been changed. Permanently. The middle class community that once resided here has been pushed to the outer boroughs, and a new class of immigrants have officially arrived. Stock brokers. Bankers. Lawyers. And with their arrival comes the slow death of diversity at the hands of gentrification. Condos have replaced landmark buildings. Mom and Pop stores have been turned into chic shops. Artist studios have given way to trendy bistros. And where people once looked to the Lower East Side for its influence on American culture and politics, they now look to this neighborhood to see where culture once was. Gaze up and down these streets my friends and take a long look. Because pretty soon . . . even once was will be gone. And as years pass the Lower East Side will become increasingly more like a museum. And more people will visit using an avatar than they will in the flesh. New York City and all its culture will officially be dead. And all that will remain . . . will be in the history books. [*Pause.*] Have a good day. [*Pause.*] Oh . . . and if you're hungry . . . we're in the heart of the pickle district. I recommend Guss'. Their full sours are to die for. Thanks again for coming.

OFFICE HOUR
Julia Cho

Dramatic
DENNIS, 18

DENNIS, *a college freshman, has been exhibiting very disturbing behavior in classes and toward other students. At the urging of her colleagues,* GINA, *one of his professors, has called him into her office to try and help him by getting to the root of the problem. This is* DENNIS's *response.*

DENNIS   The way I am is a rational response to the situation I'm in. Do you get that? You couldn't bear being me for one day. One second. No one could. You think: I must've done something. To deserve this. But you think back to when you were a *child*, when you were blank and innocent and had done *nothing* and still, *still* you were treated like shit—The way other children treated me: *There was no reason for it.* I did nothing. I *was pure.* So you realize: We're animals. We're worse than animals. Animals don't treat each other like this. They don't *degrade* each other, *wound* each other. All my life, the only thing anyone's ever told me is: I'm the problem. From day one: I'm what's wrong. And I believed them. I was just a kid so of course I believed them. I was even relieved. Thank God. Someone was going to fix me. What I have, this feeling I carry, I don't have to keep carrying it. So years and years of art therapy and speech therapy and therapy therapy. Nothing took the feeling away. Nothing took the feeling away. Nothing made life any less painful. And then you know what? I finally figured it out. Figured out what was really going on. What must be going on. *I'm* not the problem. I'm not the problem and I never was. *They* were the problem. The skulls grinning on the streets; the death heads driving their cars; the morons; the idiots; the unenlightened; the oblivious. Why was I trying so hard to fix myself? Why was I trying so hard to change? *They* weren't trying. The world is full of people who don't give a shit. So why should I? Look at me. *Look.* I didn't ask to be born this way, but here I am. I was born to be kicked. That's my function. Society needs people like me just as much as it needs the leaders, the celebrities, the admired. I should be *thanked.* I should be given an award. Without people like me, civilization would *break down.* You all should be grateful I exist.

THE PASSPORT
Arthur M. Jolly

Comic
DAN, 20s–30s

A lighter moment in an otherwise dramatic play, DAN *is talking to his boyfriend,* RAFE, *as he reluctantly packs for a trip he'd rather not take.*

DAN   Orlando. The week of fun. Theme parks force feeding fun down your throat like a Strasbourg goose, 'til you're choking on it. That is the one thing I . . . [*Beat.*] How can that not be fun? An entire industry dedicated to the concept that there can never be too much fun. An amusement park. Not joy, they're not joy parks or ecstasy parks or enlightenment parks . . . amusement. They amuse. . . . They should have a bemusement park—you don't actually go on any rides, they'd just have like an interesting-to-look at roller coaster. You just stare at it and go: hmm. [*Beat.*] Right? [*Beat.*] Harry Potter world! Best example—that was the best part of the whole week, the whole Orlando slam-fest, every goddamn park in seven days surfeit of fun. Harry Potter world. Good roller coaster? It's the same damn one they've had for years. The new ride? Okay, nothing to write—It's Hogwarts! Up on the hill, and the dragon skeleton hanging from the—that was the best part. Who cares about the ride at the end, it's walking around and seeing all those . . . amusements. It's the anticipation. We could go to Orlando. Screw the train up to Scotland, you take a couple extra days, we pack our things, find your passport and we use it. Back to the States. Orlando. Get some sun, look at a real castle, not the Scottish . . . sad stone lumps. You know what I mean—a castle with a ride in it. Fiberglass and dragons and a decent mai tai. Somewhere it's sunny. [*Beat.*] This place is so drab.

A PIECE OF PROPERTY
Richard Vetere

Seriocomic
NICK, early 30s

NICK, *an attorney, is speaking to* CHARLIE, *explaining to him that now that he owns property (ten yards by five yards, next to a bus stop), he will need someone to protect him from con men.*

NICK   A man in your position should have very shiny shoes. A man in your position should have people going out of their way to make him feel comfortable. You are a man of position now. I bet you don't know this, but the vast majority of people in the world do *not* own property. Many people do not own their own homes, their own land. You deserve the prestige you are going to get. Understand this, there will be many creepy, sharp, con-men and cheaters who will be at your doorstep trying to make money on your prestige. They will come from out of nowhere, in the middle of the night with phone calls, letters, invitations, just to get a little piece of the piece *you* have. I warn you, Charlie, don't trust those people. Teach yourself to recognize a creep and con-man when you see one. Don't let their flattery and their nice clothes trick you into thinking they are someone you can trust. Don't trust anyone but yourself, and you will do okay. Remember that. Don't trust anyone! [*Pause.*] Now, there will be a few people who you can allow into your inner circle. And these people should not be any lowlifes, or car mechanics. They should be people you would recognize immediately. They should be well-dressed, and on your side. They will deserve your confidence. Of course, it will be difficult to tell the difference between the con-man and the friend. Hire someone to help you distinguish between the two. Hire someone with intelligence and style. Pay him good money to keep the riff-raff from your door step. Feed him, and buy him nice things. Give him a title, too. Call him—your attorney. That's good. Call him, your lawyer! That will keep the riff-raff away. That will instill fear into the con-man and the thief. In fact, I know just the man you can hire. He is honest, well-educated and he dresses very well. [*Pause.*] You are looking at him, Charlie! Hire *me*!

PIRANDELLO
Don Nigro

Seriocomic
IL DUCE, 60s

The playwright LUIGI PIRANDELLO, *author of many plays that challenge our view of what reality is and what truth is, is writing on the stage of his theatre late at night, when he is visited by* IL DUCE, *who is Benito Mussolini, the Italian Fascist dictator.* IL DUCE *wants* PIRANDELLO *to write a flattering biographical play about him, but* PIRANDELLO, *who is for his own purposes a member of the Fascist Party but has no desire to do any such thing, has been trying to avoid this assignment by explaining that his plays are more about the nature of reality than they are biographies of great leaders. In the midst of these Pirandellan comments about the elusive nature of reality,* IL DUCE, *who is not used to being messed with, cuts him off with this brutal suggestion. He follows it by suggesting that he's joking, but he isn't. He is a brutal tyrant with a huge ego, but he has a dark sense of humor and a certain amount of charm, and he is determined to get what he wants, one way or the other.*

IL DUCE   How about if we chop off your dick? Would that be real enough for you?

[*Pause.*]

Relax. I'm joking. Well, sort of. Although it's amazing how effective threatening to cut off somebody's dick can be in resolving their questions about the nature of reality. But no pressure. I'm actually a very sensitive, artistic sort of fellow. I play the violin and love opera. Really. I like nothing better than listening to fat people howling at each other and pretending to die while wearing silly hats. I listen to *Pagliacci* over and over until my ears bleed. And I'm also an actor. I play the part of Il Duce. I wear a mask. But when I take my mask off, my face comes with it, and there's nothing left but a grinning skull. Or just an empty space, like the Invisible Man. Except for a nose. I might just be a nose, floating in the void. What am I supposed to do with a playwright's dick, anyway? I'm just presuming you even have a dick. Maybe instead of cutting off your dick, I could just shoot you in the elbow. Is that fair? And don't tell me a great man like myself wouldn't stoop to shooting a playwright in the elbow. I'm Il Duce. It's my duty to shoot people in the elbows. And if you can't write without your elbow, I can get D'Annunzio to write a play about me. D'Annunzio has kissed my ass so many times, his mustache smells like dog shit. Not that I've spent a lot of time smelling D'Annunzio's mustache. But I have stepped in a lot of shit. Politics is a dunghill, and I am the cock who crawls to the top and crows. Who said that? Did I say that? Am I quoting myself again? I don't even know anymore.

PIRANDELLO

Don Nigro

Dramatic
PIRANDELLO, 60s

LUIGI PIRANDELLO, *the great Italian playwright, has been writing late at night on the stage of his theatre when he is visited by a number of people who've been important in his life and who may or may not be part of the play he is trying to write. Here he is speaking to a much younger actress with whom he is desperately in love. He is unhappily married to a ferociously jealous woman he believes to be mad, and is very lonely and unhappy, but when this actress came to his hotel room late at night and offered herself to him, he was very much tempted but did the right thing and said he couldn't: because he was married, and because it would ruin their working relationship, and because she would not, in the end, be happy with a man so much older than her. But ever since that night, he has been unable to get the actress out of his mind and now wishes he'd accepted her offer of love and comfort. But now she has the upper hand and refuses to have anything to do with him, and a part of her, as a sort of revenge, seems to enjoy torturing him.*

PIRANDELLO   I think about you all the time. I write to keep
from going mad. I dream about you. Sometimes in my
dreams you love me. I go to your room and hold you in my
arms and I'm so happy. But then I wake up and you're not
there and I can't stop sobbing like a child. But in most of my
dreams you're looking at me, in a doorway, as if you're deciding whether to come to me, to give yourself to me, or to go.
And you start to come to me. But then you hear something,
over your shoulder, behind you, a voice from another room,
and you turn your back on me and close the door, and I want
to go after you, but I can't move. Or I'm in the theatre. I'm
watching a performance, from backstage. And you're there,

on stage, looking so beautiful. And I want to go onstage and rescue you from the audience, because I know they can't be trusted and will hurt you, turn on you, eventually, inevitably, because an audience is a mob without a soul. But someone is holding me back. I don't know if it's my father, or Mussolini, or who it is, but they're telling me, don't go out there. Nothing is real out there. Nothing is real. And then I'm back in that hotel room, and it's the middle of the night, and the solitude is horrible, and I know that I'm alone, and I'll always be alone, I'll die alone, and I'll never see you again. Why must reality be only one thing? I want the reality in which I never let you leave that room. And now you continue to punish me over and over again for the terrible sin of trying to behave like a decent person. When an old man loves a young woman, he deserves all the humiliation he gets. But I can't seem to help it. It's like I've been cast in a role and I can't get out of it. Sometimes I feel so much love it just overwhelms me. I can't think straight, and I can't seem to control what I say or do. Things just fly out of my mouth like bats out of a cave. I feel too much.

PLAYING WITH FIRED
Steven Hayet

Comic
RONALD, mid-40s

RONALD, *a widower, finds out that he's just been fired from his dream job, Senior Assistant Director of Product Distribution for J.C. Toys.*

RONALD   So I'm fired? Just like that?

[*Beat.*]

> When I got this job, I was so excited I called every relative, every friend, everyone I knew to say "Hey, look at me. I'm going to be working at J.C. Toys: Number 31 on Fortune Magazine's Best 100 Companies to Work For. I had reached the top third of the mountain!" And now, after two weeks of me busting my rump—arriving early, staying late, working through lunch—you are going to give me some cock and bull story about "greater good." Let me tell you this: you may view me as just an easily replaceable cog in a machine, but I loved being a cog. I loved knowing that this machine ran because of something I did- even if the overall impact of my job was . . .

[*Collecting himself.*]

> I mean, I get it. I'm only the Senior Assistant Director of Product Distribution at a toy manufacturer. It's not like I'm Santa Claus, but I was okay with that. As a kid on Christmas, I always would think of the elves. Children leave out cookies for Santa and carrots for the reindeer, yet the elves behind the scenes never get thanks. No kid opens a present and says "Oh thank you, Elves!" but without elves, there is no Christmas. I'm sorry I wasn't a good enough elf.

PRESERVATION

Deborah Yarchun

Seriocomic
STAN, late 30s

STAN *is speaking to* LYDIA, *also late 30s, in the atrium of an archival library where he works. It's their second encounter. Earlier that week,* LYDIA *confronted* STAN *in the back room with her belief that Avram, the late founder of the archival library (who was revered and allegedly celibate), is her grandfather.* LYDIA *has returned and informed* STAN *that her grandmother passed away yesterday and insists Avram lied.*

STAN   You shouldn't go around saying things—like you're saying—people believe things. Without evidence. They believe things. You think this place pays for itself with just his money? It's seed funds. The place is supported by donors. Do you have any idea how much it costs to run an archival library? You think a public library is at risk? A private library is ALWAYS at risk. The whole place is hanging by a hair. Which I guess is ironic because he didn't have any. Listen, I've started to lose my own, because of the stress of it. I've thought about collecting it. Sticking it in a baggy and preserving it in a vault. Archivist's former hair. Evidence I once had some. Or maybe if you live in a vault long enough—you start to lose it. Avram was honest. People know him as an honest, giving man. And he was. A seminal figure. A germinal figure. And he was funny—"A bald head leaves more room for the brain to breathe." People aren't just investing in the library, they're investing in him. In his legacy and his ideas. I was raised by them, okay? They're good and I genuinely believe in him. And he was GOOD. He wouldn't have done that. He was a wealthy benefactor, poet, artist and holy man. He was NOT a scoundrel. This is his temple. Have some respect. The man who raised me was not kind. But Avram was. I've devoted my life to him. I know you're mourning. But all you're proving is that if anybody achieves a modicum of goodness in the world, there's somebody out for blood.

QUEER THEORY
Brooke Berman

Dramatic
JORGE, late 30s

JORGE *tells the audience about his eventual death.*

JORGE   I will die in my apartment. Not in the timeline of this
play. Years later. But eventually. Here. Someone will find me. I
never married, I wasn't in a relationship. I was alone. Which is
nothing to sneer at or feel bad about. I liked being alone. I had
a lot of boyfriends after Wes. And hookups. And eventually
once it was invented, Grindr dates. But essentially I was alone
and I liked it like that. So when I die in my rent controlled East
Village apartment, my body lies there alone for a while before
it is discovered. By a neighbor with a key. Who wonders about
the smell and why she hasn't seen me come or go for a few
days. It's awful. But she's all right. She can take it. She knows
who to call and they come take care of it and my sister comes
down from Rhode Island with her kids and my brother comes
in from New Jersey with his and our parents are long gone
themselves so—someone thinks to call Wes. Who is promot-
ing a film. But Wes has a very appropriate reaction. He breaks
down crying. I was his one true love. I was. Despite many
boyfriends before and after I will remain the one who showed
him what True Love's Kiss could do. And that's quite an honor.
I relish having been that person. I am so happy to have played
the role.

[*As if performing.*]

In this evening's performance, the role of True Love's Kiss will
be played by Jorge Cortes.

[*As if receiving an award.*]

Thank you. It was a role I treasured.

RIGHT PLACE, RIGHT TIME
Lia Romeo

Seriocomic
MARK, mid-20s

MARK *is speaking to* STEPHANIE, *his ex-fiancée. He stood her up at the altar, but now he's returned to try to explain himself.*

MARK   I got scared. I didn't know if I was ready for this kind of commitment. But you were so amazing, and I got so swept away . . . and then when you went back home I started to panic—and the day I was going to fly here to meet you I flew to Vegas instead. And I figured out that you're exactly what I want for the rest of my life. Because I hired an escort. [*Beat.*] I hired a few escorts. [*Beat.*] I hired forty escorts and we had a party. Me and the escorts. It lasted all night. And at one point around four a.m. I had three of them and they were all, you know, doing different things to me, and I kept looking back and forth between these escorts and all I could see was your face. The most beautiful escorts in Vegas . . . huge, naked tits bouncing in my face . . . hot, wet tongues licking my . . . you get the idea. The point is, all I could think about was you. And that's when I realized how much I loved you. How I didn't want anyone else—at least not very often. So here I am. [*Beat.*] Steffie, please. I'll never go to an escort again—I'll never even look at an escort—I'll never even look at a regular woman! I love you so much!

RIGHT PLACE, RIGHT TIME
Lia Romeo

Dramatic
RICHARD, 40

RICHARD *is speaking to* STEPHANIE, *with whom he's accidentally fallen in love after entering into a marriage of convenience.*

RICHARD   I don't want you to sleep with Mark—or anyone else. I want to have you and hold you and love you and cherish you till death do us part. What Linda and I used to have—I didn't care where I was as long as she was there. And when she wasn't, I could be anywhere in the world and it wouldn't be any good without her. I believe in happy endings. I know I didn't get one the first time around, but I still believe someday I will. I doubted it for a while, but you've brought this feeling, this love back into my heart, and it feels too good for me to believe it won't end somewhere wonderful. I know we haven't known each other long, and I know it's probably crazy to think a girl like you would ever fall for someone like me— but I wonder if maybe eventually you might be able to love me too. [*Beat.*] I want something perfect. I'm forty years old and I'm divorced and I'm losing my hair and I ought to know better, but I want something perfect. I don't want to settle for what I can get.

THE ROMEO AND JULIET OF SARAJEVO
Brian Silberman

Dramatic
ZIJO ISMIC, mid-40s, Bosnian Muslim

Admira Ismic and Bosko Brkic were natives of the former Yugoslavia living in Sarajevo during the Bosnian War. She was a Muslim and he a Catholic Serb, but the young couple fell in love. They were killed on May 19, 1993, while attempting to escape their war-torn city. Photographs of their bodies were used by media outlets and a Reuters dispatch was filed dubbing them the Romeo and Juliet of Sarajevo. Here, ZIJO ISMIC—Admira's father—speaks to a Bosnian official in the United Nations Protection Force. (The theatrical conceit is that he is speaking in his native language.)

ISMIC   I'm not asking for choosing sides. I'm just asking for an armored truck for me to drive. I don't care who killed them, I just want Admira and Bosko so I can bury them. I don't want them to rot in no-man's land. [*There is a slight pause.*] Their bags disappeared last night. Did you know? We get reports from ham radio. They snuck up close and grabbed their bags with hooks because they thought there would be big money in them. Because there was saying around town that they had 100,000 Deutschmarks. And for five days they lie there. Hungry dogs and cats roving on the streets and they're in the middle of downtown. It's a hot May for Sarajevo . . . in the heat and on the street and we're not able to do anything. Their bodies are being doused in petrol and hit with Molotov cocktails and they were shooting incendiary bullets to try to burn them, trying to destroy the bodies so there's no evidence. Nothing to say which side had fired at them. UNPRO-FOR will help us, we say. Everyone says. UNPROFOR is there for humanitarian issues. They must do that because they're paid to do that. Foreign journalists, they tell us this. Reuters.

The wire. I'll drive. None of your men will have to take the risk. *I'll* do it. I'll take the risk alone. I'm her father. I'll get the bodies and bring them back.

THE ROMEO AND JULIET OF SARAJEVO
Brian Silberman

Dramatic
ZIJO ISMIC, mid-40s, Bosnian Muslim

Admira Ismic and Bosko Brkic were natives of the former Yugoslavia living in Sarajevo during the Bosnian War. She was a Muslim and he a Catholic Serb, but the young couple fell in love. They were killed on May 19, 1993, while attempting to escape their war-torn city. Photographs of their bodies were used by media outlets and a Reuters dispatch was filed dubbing them the Romeo and Juliet of Sarajevo. Here, ZIJO ISMIC—Admira's father—speaks to the audience after their death. (The theatrical conceit is that he is speaking in his native language.)

ISMIC   What they say . . . about Bosko . . . is that it is he who is the gentle one. That my Admira, she works on cars. She is tough. That I treat her as boy because I make work her in a garage and she likes to be mechanic. But what *I* think. I think you do not know. I think you do not know these things like what I know. And that it is not fair. And it is not the right thing. [*He pauses slightly.*] Bosko, he knows some people that if you knew them, some of these people, you would not say he is the gentle one. And perhaps he has done some not gentle things too, I don't know. All I know . . . at first I come garage in a morning and the cars they would be different. In different place. A little bit. But different from where I leave them. I see this things. Is only me with a key. And Admira. And there is no breaking into. Is not thief. I see this things and first I say nothing. But then I ask her one day. Admira. And she is good girl. She loves her father. Is Bosko asking of her. Is Admira.opening garage at night for cars to drive. They go to steal from UNPROFOR. Petrol and other things to sell on black market. Is Bosko. And Misa Cuk. Maybe my

Admira too. Stealing. They take and put in the cars and then drive around selling. And I say nothing. Is *dangerous*. There are bad people. To do this you are with bad people. But I say nothing. I only look each day I open garage and see the cars still being different. [*He pauses*.] I am a father. Is the father's job to protect his child. And things I am hearing. Maybe I am not good father. Maybe I am not. There are bad people. And maybe it is not Serb Srpska *or* Army of Republic who shoot them. Maybe it is not. You see? Is the cars. Is the dangerous Black Market people Bosko bring to my Admira. [*He takes a step forward*.] So, do not say Bosko is always the gentle one. Maybe they are dying and it is *him*. Yes? Maybe it is all his fault. [*There is a slight pause*.] That is what I want to say.

THE SABBATH GIRL
Cary Gitter

Dramatic
SETH, 32

SETH, *an Orthodox Jew who runs a knish store on the Lower East Side of Manhattan, confesses his love to* ANGIE, *30, the Italian American woman who lives down the hall from him.*

SETH   My crisis of faith? Well, Angie, I guess it has to do with when I knocked on Mr. Lee's door back in June and *you* answered? And I thought I had the wrong apartment, but I didn't. It was just that *you* had moved in. And I knew I was there to ask you to turn on my AC, because it was the Sabbath and I wasn't allowed to, but . . . I couldn't stop looking at your smile? Which is somehow a little sad at the same time as it's happy? Like you can see you've been disappointed by a lot of stuff, but you still have all kinds of hope because that's just your nature? And in the background I saw your work laid out on the table and your wine and your Ritz crackers and I thought, "This is how she spends her Friday nights. What a *mensch*." And I haven't talked to a lot of people—I mean really *talked*—in the last couple of years, but talking to you somehow feels like the easiest, most familiar thing in the world? And you told me about your loneliness. And I understand that. And you care so much about your work. And I understand that too. And today when you showed up at the store, in your dress, and I gave you a knish and you took that first bite, I felt, I don't know, I felt happy, Angie! Okay? What can I say? I'm not a happy person at all—far from it—I'm still reeling from a bad marriage and a break from my community—but I felt like the happiest man on earth watching you eat that knish! Watching you enjoy something so much. Something *I* gave you. And I thought to myself, "What if I could just keep making Angie happy? Wouldn't that be nice?" So I don't know. I don't know. I mean you're one thing and I'm something else, and that's like an enormous—But I am having a crisis of faith, Angie, and to be perfectly and completely honest with you, you are a primary cause of it. So I don't know what to do. But that's the truth. The *emmis*.

SÁME

Ron Riekki

Dramatic
NILS, 40s

NILS, *a nontraditional student taking a course entitled Islam and Media, is presenting a summation of his final essay to the class, but after several interruptions from another student, he finds himself delivering his paper with a passion even he did not expect.*

NILS   So why the Great Lakes?

[*He looks to see if anyone will answer.*]

Swing states! Exceptionally tight swing states. And so why market Islamophobia to these swing state Great Lakes voters? Because it taps into a fear that can be particularly exploited in the Great Lakes region. All semester long we've been saying East-West, East-West; everything's "East-West," as if there's no such thing as North and South. I'm telling you right now, we have to start including North and South in discussions of the world. There is an Africa and there is an Arctic, but, listen—OK, so Illinois is considered to be the "most Muslim state" per capita in the U.S., as reported by the *Huffington Post*. OK. With New York, Michigan, and Pennsylvania in the top ten, so half the Great Lakes states are in the top ten for Islamic population . . . Ontario, also Great Lakes, and if we include Québec in the discussion, then we're talking about more than a million Muslims living in that region. Great Lakes region. For Canada, realize that just over seventy-eight percent of all of Canada's Muslims live in Ontario or Québec. Combined, the U.S. and Canada have over fifty percent of their Islamic population in the Great Lakes. Double what population demographics would expect. This large Muslim presence has meant a potentially exploitable Islamophobia if marketed properly—and let's be honest, Islamophobia is marketed with the same brutal repetition of Geico and Coke. Or the Koch brothers. And this Islamophobia was tapped during the election. Trump did this. Where was Trump's mammoth news-getting "radical Islamic terrorism" speech given? In Youngstown, *Ohio*. In the heart of the Great Lakes region . . . During the White House Correspondents' Dinner, where did Trump hold his rally? Harrisburg, *Pennsylvania*. Look, Trump is going to keep rallying in the Great Lakes throughout the next four years, because he wants to get reelected. The next election is going to be decided in the Great Lakes. I had a Jewish Studies class here where they were saying that the real land of the Jews was the Atlantic, that the "Jewish Atlantic"—but it's not. It's the *Jewish Great Lakes*. That's where—the Underground Railroad, the whole—Look, she—my instructor for that class said, "You're not going to find Jews in Minnesota" and I said, did you know that there's—if you dis—if you don't factor in Israel and treat Minnesota as a *country*, it would be in the top ten in the world for Jewish population. And there's not any Jews there? *The Midwest is the Middle East.*

SHERLOCK HOLMES AND THE ADVENTURE OF THE ELUSIVE EAR

David MacGregor

Comic
DR. WATSON, 30s–50s

DR. WATSON *is frustrated with* SHERLOCK HOLMES *as lately*
HOLMES *hasn't given him anything interesting to write about.*

WATSON   Right. You listen to me, Holmes! I know how much
you're in love with your own cleverness, but I've been meaning to have a word about the state of affairs in this house-
hold! Now then, I am well aware of just how stupid I am. I get
daily reminders from you about how mind-numbingly slow
and thick I must be because I can't solve murders based on
the depth to which the parsley has sunk into the butter on a
hot summer day. However, despite my vast and apparently
unending ignorance, may I point out that I am the only one
here actually making money. I get paid fifty pounds for every
story of yours I write up in *The Strand Magazine*. When was
the last time you got paid for a case? And no, don't you dare
say, "the work is its own reward." No, it isn't! *Money* is its own
reward! Pounds, sovereigns, half crowns. A bloody farthing,
for God's sake! I'm the only one paying the bills and your
most recent cases haven't given me a bloody thing to write
about! I mean . . .

[*Pulling out his notebook.*]

. . . just listen to these. Last Thursday, Mrs. Pickford of 73 Go-
van Lane lost her cat, Mr. Jingles. You cleverly retrieved the
cat from a dustbin where it had fallen asleep. You followed
up this triumph when Mr. Hainsely of 14 Broadchurch Road
reported his wife missing and suspected murdered, and
you found her in the alley behind her usual pub in a drunk-

en stupor and brought her home. And just yesterday, Lady Claybourne's supposedly stolen emerald necklace was found in the pocket of her own nightgown, where she had forgotten she put it because she's getting a bit senile. You see the problem? I can't possibly write up any of those as a new adventure! You think people want to sit down and read "The Adventure of the Sleeping Pussycat"? "The Adventure of the Not Actually Stolen Jewelry"? We need something with an edge! Something foreign, dangerous, a master criminal, like Professor Moriarty! The Napoleon of Crime! Sitting like a giant spider at the center of London's underworld, plotting and scheming the most bizarre and outlandish crimes imaginable. That's precisely what we need! Except someone in this room, and I'm not pointing fingers, someone in this room threw him off a waterfall! In other words Holmes, and I can't put it any more plainly, I'm not saying that psychopathic criminals don't have their downside, but they're a damned sight more interesting than sleeping pussycats!

SKIN HUNGRY
Erin Mallon

Comic
ROWAN, 23

ROWAN *is talking to* JIM, *whose 74 year-old mother,* RUTH, *he is dating.*

ROWAN Can I do that thing no one ever wants you to do where I show you picture of a baby I love deeply who you don't particularly care about but need to show intense interest in or else you run the risk of appearing like an unfeeling asshole? Great! This is Raina, my niece. She's a month old. I went to meet her the week after she was born. I brought my brother and his wife a Tupperware container filled with Beefaroni. I love Beefaroni and apparently putting food in a Tupperware container really hits it home to the new parents that you care. I googled "how to support new parents" and learned that little tidbit. Oh and for the record, you're not supposed to ask for the Tupperware back. Just let 'em keep it, so make sure it's not something you're too attached to. Anyway, I get there and they get me all propped up with pillows on their fancy couch, then they plop little Raina in my arms. And know what she did? Her little hand instantly wrapped around my finger. Tight. Like she trusted me. Like she knew I was good people. Knew she was safe with me. I was so moved and grateful, I almost cried all over her little baby body. Meant a lot to me, ya know? Like she's the only person besides my mom, and now Ruth, who doesn't always assume I'm a fuck up.

SKIN HUNGRY
Erin Mallon

Comic
ROWAN, 23

ROWAN *is out to dinner with his 74-year-old girlfriend*, RUTH; *her disapproving 43-year-old son*, JIM; *and* JIM's *cuddle therapist*, GINA. *Things are tense. Everyone is drinking wine.*

ROWAN   You a hand washer? Great. Hashtag Me too. [*Beat.*] Ya know, I'm realizing that I don't always say the right thing. And ya know, I think it gets in my way? People have a real easy time dismissing me as just some dippy kid. Because I say such stupid shit, man! But here's the thing: I don't even know it's perceived negatively until it's out in the open, like . . . wafting around and offending everyone. [*Quick beat.*] It's like . . . do you ever catch a whiff of your armpit and it shocks you? Like

[*He sniffs his pit.*]

you just can't believe that that smell is coming from you because you thought you were relatively clean? It's like that. I think I love her man. And I know what you were all insinuating back there, thinking that losing my mom is what draws me to Ruth. But that's some bullshit. Situations couldn't be more different. I miss my mom and like being her son, but your mom? Your mom makes me want to run through a big field, tear my shirt open then roll around in the dirt until it gets stuck in all the cracks and creases of my body so anybody who takes one look at me would be like "Wow, you've had a day, huh?" She makes me wanna jump into a big ass body of water, squish the sandy bottom with my big toes, then gather a shit ton of seashells and make necklaces for all my friends. She makes me wanna jump out of a car while it's still moving.

SNORE
Max Posner

Dramatic
ABE, 26

ABE *is an angry and disillusioned employee of a virtuous peace-building nonprofit in a large city. At a birthday party, ABE's college best friend, TOM, encourages him to describe the wonders of his job to the new boyfriend of another friend. Drunkenly, ABE reveals that he has quit his job and lays bare the full extent of his despair.*

ABE   They bring a lot of kids from Palestine and Israel and from India and Pakistan, from different warring places, and put the kids in like these little outdoorsy camps in Minnesota, and they go on hikes together and do ropes courses and some of them probably make out, and they learn the same songs and tell stories about each others' grandparents and they make fires together and they stay up late and play pranks on each other. So they take them there and they start erasing all the lines between them imposed by culture and government and religion, they wring the hatred right out of them and these Israeli boys have these little Palestinian girlfriends and these Pakistani girls are staying up late hearing these Indian girls talk about their grandmothers and their struggles, and the counselors are all like us—Aside from getting these kids to think they're all the same and then sending them home to a place where the Palestinians are still throwing rocks at their tanks and the Israelis are still bulldozing their pets into pieces. Last month at the camp these two kids got lost on a hike and we never found them, and you know I thought the whole organization would end, would formally apologize and close up shop, but they just tried really hard to explain themselves and avoid terrible law suits, and somehow they did, and they kept it out of the news and everything, and no one knows about it and we're "in the clear" but it's like two kids are just fucking gone, and why? Where? And I'm supposed to like keep writing grants?

SQUEAKY
Jeff Cohen

Dramatic
JEFF, 50

JEFF *is dealing with end-of-life issues with his dad,* STAN "SQUEAKY" COHEN, *and is speaking to his older brother* ROB, *with whom he has a somewhat dysfunctional relationship.*

JEFF   I know the past is the past and I know you think I'm being an asshole but look, Rob, all I'm saying is that I'm worried about Stan. You don't know what goes on—like when his cancer doctor calls to tell me he isn't gonna treat him anymore because there's a deductible that Medicare doesn't cover which our father of course refuses to pay and now he owes ten thousand dollars and I have to come down and find out they told Stan to buy this cheap supplemental insurance that covers the deductible but Stan refuses to do it. Stan starts yelling *that's what Medicare is for* and the *doctor is just trying to rip me off*. This is for his prostate cancer, he needs a shot every six months. I say to the book-keeper there *what if Stan buys the medicine himself—would the doctor just give him the shot*? The doctor agrees and now Stan has to arrange to buy the medicine from a pharmacy at $3000 a pop and then he has to wait three months for Medicare to reimburse him but what the fuck [*Sarcastic.*] thank god he doesn't have to buy supplemental insurance. [*Beat.*] One time I come down and take Stan to buy the medicine and we get up to the Doctor's office and Stan starts looking in all his pockets—he doesn't have the medicine. *Where is it, Stan? I don't know, Jeff.* We retrace our steps—I'm thinking maybe he dropped it. We tear the car apart looking for it. Nothing. I call the pharmacy to see if maybe he'd left it on the counter or something, but he didn't. Stan starts panicking, starts crying and now he's walking aimlessly around the parking lot in the pouring rain. Rob, I swear to you I've never seen anyone look so bewildered and old. I don't know what the fuck to do so I go over and try to give him a hug and I say to him *it'll be alright, Stan, I promise. Worse comes to worse, we'll just buy more medicine.* [*Beat.*] And then, out of the corner of my eye, I see one of those big trash receptacles in the parking lot. And it hits me. When we were leaving his house, Connie had given Stan a bag of household trash to throw away and I start thinking . . . and I go over to the garbage can and reach into it—it's all wet from the rain, it's disgusting—and I pull out the garbage bag that Connie had given to Stan and I look inside and there is Stan's medicine. [*Beat.*] And that's what I'm trying to tell you. He can't function on his own anymore. And I want to be his guardian.

TENANTS
Nat Cassidy

Dramatic
JEFF, 30–40

M and G move into a new apartment, only to find JEFF, the previous tenant, increasingly trying to insinuate himself into their lives. Here he makes a speech at their housewarming party he crashed.

JEFF Happy Warm House. Welcome to the neighborhood. This is a really great neighborhood. I have lived here a long time. And, y'know, this world is, is a cold, deep crater of shit. But not with people like M and G. They have moved here and, and I'm just so happy. Um. There is an exhibit at the museum right now, it's amazing, all about There's this hornet, the Japanese giant hornet, big as my thumb! Spits poison! Horrifying! And, and that's the kind of world we live in, guys. And these hornets, they can massacre entire colonies of European honeybees, right? M and G? You know this, right? They just slice them in half with their jaws like an assembly line until the ground is literally carpeted. But that's the European honeybees. The *Japanese* honeybees . . . this is their *home*. They know how to protect their hive, they know, because . . . So, when the hornets, when they send a scout out to look for beehives, the Japanese honeybees all know to hide. To draw the hornet inside, and then what they all know to do next is amazing, they all land on top of the hornet, all of them, and they start rubbing their legs together. They can't pierce his armor, they know this, and you can see 'em, they do thermal imaging of them. They immobilize the intruder . . . and then they cook it. Roast it. To death. Within like one degree of their own lives. And isn't that incredible? Home is a very important thing. A strengthening thing. When you're home, you can do anything. So to M and G: welcome home.

TROLLING 101
Brenton Lengel

Comic
TROLL, could be any age but probably in his 20s

An internet TROLL *explains himself in a direct address to the audience.*

TROLL   It is common to think that we Internet Trolls are a new. Phenomenon. Brought on. By the anonymity of cyberspace. This is incorrect. And those who believe it—

[*He glances at the audience, disapprovingly.*]

Are *prejudiced.* In fact, we trolls have been around for *OVER 9,000* years!!! The very first mythical troll. Was Lucifer. Who, after being banhammered from heaven, proceeded to troll two humans named Adam and Eve . . . Successfully. I'm sure you've heard of it. It is a very popular fairytale. Trolling is a style of rhetoric, which can be used . . . for a variety of purposes. Socrates was known to employ. The troll method . . . The Internet. Is just a convenient platform. Upon which to. Share our ideas. Trollin' is 'a' art! No, I'm waxing poetic . . . *trolling is a science!* The reason trolls find the Internet so. Attractive is that unlike the polite society of your meatspace, in the cold vacuum of cyberspace. Feelings. Don't matter. Opinions. Don't matter. You. Don't matter. Only the hard survive the Internet! Only the strong! Some trolls. Are made. But. The best Trolls. Are born. And therefore the United States should implement a system of nationalized eugenics, in order to create a master race. OF TROLLS! [*Beat.*] You're being Trolled. Today we witness the miracle of birth!

TV IN MY BONES

C. S. Hanson

Comic
NARRATOR, 30s, any gender

The NARRATOR *sets up each short play in this evening of quirky stories that reflect TV's ability to unite us, divide us, pervade our culture, suck our time, and by all means entertain us. The* NARRATOR *takes the stage with grand gestures, for he/she is the Master/Mistress of Ceremonies. Following is the* NARRATOR's *opening for the show.*

NARRATOR   Ladies and gentlemen, please take a moment to turn on your streaming devices. That's right. You heard me. Turn on your cell phones, your tablets, your laptops and whatever goes beep. All your mobile devices. Take 'em out, turn them on, volume LOUD. Feel free to stream your favorite shows. Take a call. Make a call. Tweet. Post. Take a selfie.

[*Addressing an audience member.*]

Sir, if that cell phone you're cradling is on MUTE, we'll have to confiscate it. People, turn your devices on. Why? Because this is TV IN YOUR BONES. We want you to feel at home.

[*Narrator puts hand to ear.*]

What? Oh, sorry. One of the producers. You know—behind a glass screen, in a booth? They see us. We don't see them.

[*Listening.*]

TV IN MY BONES? Are you sure? . . . Oh, okay.

[*To audience.*]

TV IN <u>MY</u> BONES. Not YOUR bones, not DEM Bones, MY bones. How about OUR bones?

[*Alarmed by the voice in ear.*]

Okay, okay. Yes, this is TV IN MY BONES. I'm your host, Alexander/Alexandra Stine. Take a call if you need to. If you get hungry, order out for snacks. We suggest using "Seamless-dot-com." Go ahead, download the app. That's "Seamless-dot-com." Life used to be so simple. Three channels. Three shows to choose from. One television for the whole family. Now you don't even need a TV to watch TV. Go ahead, sir, put on your headphones and watch Home Improvement. We don't mind. What are you really looking for deep down? Someone to watch TV with for the rest of your life? Is TV part of the glue that keeps relationships together? TV sets us up. Gives us expectations for what we think we want in life. Even my plants love a happy ending. I don't water them anymore. I just turn on Jessica Jones and they perk right up. But what if life doesn't turn out the way we expect it to? Where do we find solace then? Let's find out. Get comfortable. Take off your shirt, your pants—no, please don't do that. Keep your clothes on, folks. That's all we ask. Now, sit back and enjoy the show!

UNTEACHABLE

Kelly Younger

Dramatic
ALEX, 19–21

ALEX *doesn't see why today's students should have to read the "Great Books," as he tells his professor.*

ALEX   So why should we be forced to take classes or read books that make us feel worse? Why should we let professors stand up there and lecture us about how great the past was when it was only old white guys like them standing around and talking about truth and beauty, while the rest of us would have been the ones hauling stones up a pyramid or something? [*Pause.*] They call us snowflakes? Or roll their eyes when we demand safe spaces? They're the ones living in safe spaces. They just don't want to share. And they act like they understand the real world, or that they get our generation and know what's best, but they have no idea what school has been like for us. You can get cyber-bullied 24/7, or if your parents didn't put you on Adderall in third grade, you're buying it now to get through finals. And they don't get that no kid after 9/11 has ever felt safe. And the safe spaces are disappearing. Concerts, churches, movie theaters. We've been doing active-shooter drills since kindergarten. We practice . . . practice for school shootings. [*Beat.*] And they wonder why we want to feel safe? [*Beat.*] But if they're so smart, and these great books are so great . . . so great that we have to keep reading them over and over . . . then why is the world so messed up? Maybe if we stopped reading these so-called classics, and started doing something . . . something real, something meaningful . . . even if just by signing this petition . . . we could do something that mattered.

WANDERERS
Anna Ziegler

Dramatic
ABE, 30s–40s

ABE is speaking here to JULIA CHEEVER, *the movie star he believes he's in love with. We are at the climax of this relationship—the moment when* ABE *feels he must finally act on his love for* JULIA—*and in doing so he is letting her in on his deepest secret: that his now-deceased mother begged him to marry his wife,* SOPHIE, *and that he never loved her—a secret that (perhaps conveniently) justifies his decision to leave* SOPHIE *for* JULIA. ABE *is tortured at this point by self-hatred, guilt, and too many conflicted emotions to count, but he's also unloading something he's kept hidden for a long time, even from himself, so there's relief in the revelation; the weight of getting it off his chest lends it incredible urgency.*

ABE [*In anguish.*] I spent years of my life, Julia, years when my parents were both *alive*, toiling over this book about a fucking *orphan*. And suddenly there I am standing in front of *Barnes and Nobles*, having just read from that *stupid* book, when my mother calls and says, I need you to come home, Abraham. My sister Leah had just had her third baby and my mother was desperate to be there. Each baby my sisters had was another huge blow, each one a reminder of everything my mother didn't have. But I was a week away from the end of the tour. And this wasn't the first time she'd asked this of me. So I told her she would have to wait. I said one week, Mameh. And I hung up . . . I mean, Sophie doesn't even know about this! How could I tell her? You see, my mother begged me to marry her. For years, she *begged* me. She loved Soph like she was her own daughter and my mother was tragically short on family for someone who so badly wanted it. She was unsubtle about it. [*With a slight Yiddish lilt.*] "Abraham, you're going to marry that girl; you want to even if you don't know it yet." She was a Jewish mother, whether she liked it or not. She was also my mother. My only mother . . . I got the call when I was on the train, somewhere between San Diego and LA. My phone buzzed in my pocket and I knew. I did. I knew. So I didn't pick up. This was one of the many times I didn't answer when my father called. I flew home. I took a cab from the airport straight to Williamsburg, straight to Sophie. It was the middle of the night. I walked up those five flights of stairs and banged on the door until she let me in. And she let me in because I let her believe I was who she wanted me to be. She let me in because she was genuinely in love with me, which is actually the hardest thing to . . . But how could I not be with her? How could I not have those children my mother so desperately wanted? Every book I ever write will be a mea culpa. Every word a reminder of that particular cruelty. No, *everything* is a reminder. The days I spend in front of blank screens when I should be . . . I mean, my kids are growing so fast I hardly recognize them. And I just . . . I don't want anyone else to die. Please. Don't let anyone else . . . I can't do it. I can't tell my wife I didn't love her the way she loved me, that I *submitted* to our marriage. I don't even want to believe it. Could there be anything sadder? But the saddest things are usually true. My mother in the darkness. The way when I look at my wife I feel such shame. You understand now.

WEST OF EDEN
Steven Keyes

Comic
VICTOR, 40s

VICTOR, *a gay man in his 40s, greets a party guest.*

VICTOR Hi. Welcome to L.A.! I'm Victor, Adam's friend and the host of this shindig. AdamAdamAdam! I *adore* Adam. We met a few months ago doing wheatgrass shots in the oxygen bar at NOD. I loooooove that place! *Everybody* goes there. All the kids go there. I'm like a sore thumb but screw 'em. I'm not gonna roll over and die just 'cause I'm past puberty. And honey, I am *so* past puberty don't *even*—though I can still get lucky every once in awhile. Especially when they get aload of this house and all. The owner of this place is a "friend with benefits" from waaay back in the *stoned*-age. Now we're just, you know, "roommates" as they say. He's Hollywood royalty. He won an Oscar back-in-the-day but got blacklisted so they only finally gave it to him a couple years ago. He keeps it in the closet. You can hold it if you want. I help him out 'cause of his being *old* and all. I'm the houseboy! [*Pause.*] Oy. Thank God for moggies. Mogadons, darling. You can't get them here but we go to London once a year and stock up. Yawanta couple? They're heaven, absolute heaven. Next stop, Dreamland woohoo! You never know when you're gonna need to check out, baby. I slept through the last earthquake and didn't wake up till the FEMA crews arrived. Consciousness is over-rated and you can quote me: Oblivia Newton-John!

WE THE PEOPLE
John Cappelletti

Dramatic
BROCK, 60

BROCK *is the founder of We the People, a group of American terrorists. He is speaking to* FRANCIS, *one of his followers, attempting to convince him to not leave the group.*

BROCK   Okay, let's take a walk. I don't like sitting too long anyway. We get comfortable with the status quo and then we just fall asleep. We've been asleep too long, like Rip Van Winkle or somebody. It's time to wake up. It's hard to imagine that We the People actually fought a revolution in this country, we're so fuckin lethargic. But I'm thinking: maybe it's time for another one. Listen, Francis, do you know who John Lewis is? He's that Congressman who worked with Martin Luther King. He said when you see something that's wrong, that's, uh, unfair, you've got to say something, **do** something, and not be quiet. That's our mission, that's why this must be done. We the People got work to do. 'Cause after we get these damn guns off the streets, we gotta replace our miserable economic system with one that'll enable families to put a roof over their heads and food on their tables. Then we've got to put a stop to corporate greed like fracking and banking and bad mortgages and Wall Street and put those upper class criminals behind bars instead of just slapping them on the wrist with fines. Then we've got to fix the Supreme Court and the Election Process, oh, God, what a mess that has been. Francis, we have a mountain to climb. But, as Tom Paine said, "These are the times that try men's souls." And "We have it in our power to begin our world over again." Ya see, once we get Congress by the balls, we can begin our world over again and return this great country to We the People, the way Washington did when he led us to freedom. And ya know, we **can** be free again. Yes, we can! Now you got me preaching again. Let's go, before I start standin' on a soapbox or a pulpit or somethin'.

WHAT HAPPENED THAT NIGHT
Lia Romeo

Dramatic
BENNY, 17

BENNY *is speaking to his friend* KATE *about what happened at a party recently.*

BENNY   I mean I do . . . care about you, Kate . . . I love you. But I'm not actually even over here because of you, not really, I'm over here because I can't . . . fucking sleep. I can't sleep, and when I do fall asleep I have these dreams, like last night I dreamed I had my stepsister in her car seat in the back of my car, and I was going to the grocery store, but then after I got some groceries I decided to walk home. And I didn't even realize she was still there in the parking lot 'til like an hour later, and I ran all the way back but the car wasn't there and the lot was just totally empty. And it's not that anything's wrong with my sister, it's—something's wrong with *you*, and I think maybe what happened to you was my fault. And I feel . . . completely . . . terrible about it, and if you felt better, if you got better, then maybe I wouldn't feel so terrible anymore. I *left* you there, Kate. You were wasted and I knew you were wasted, and I love you but when you're wasted you get really fucking annoying. You were . . . loud, and you were talking, and I knew at some point you were going to be crying, and I was having a shitty night because I'd been having this really interesting conversation with Frank and then he somehow started making out with Adele Cummings, and I was just like I don't want to deal with it. 'Cause every time you get wasted I listen to you cry and I get you home safe and I call you in the morning, and I was just like *I* want to cry, I know that's so pathetic, but I want to be the one who's crying, not the one who's always trying to comfort someone else. So I went home and I cried for a little bit and then I went to bed, and I woke up and I had a text from Kristen about how drunk you'd been, and that's when I started to get worried. I always take care of you, Kate. I always take care of you and I left you, and this is what happened.

WHAT SCREAMS I HEAR ARE MINE
Annalise Cain

Dramatic
NILS, 20s

After overhearing a rape in her building, fourteen-year-old DANA investigates it, to the dismay of her guardian and older sister MIRA-BELLE and NILS, their handyman. Through many trials and tribulations, DANA discovers that NILS raped MIRABELLE. Cornered by an enraged sister, NILS must defend the indefensible.

NILS   LISTEN TO ME! SHE DOESN'T REMEMBER! Dana, she doesn't remember it! She blacked out—and I cleaned her up, I put her in bed, I want to *fix this*! I know what I did was awful, but I know you can forgive me. Ok, that wasn't me—I didn't do that in my right mind, it's like when someone's drunk and they say something mean or stupid, you forgive them, they aren't REALLY conscious. If I was conscious, if I didn't drink anything that night, I would let you hurt me. If I had done that completely sober, I would be an evil person. People are defined by their actions, right? And if their actions are out of their control, then that's not them! I know what I've—I should be held responsible, but I can be forgiven! And—and I shouldn't be persecuted for wanting something everyone else wants —I love Mirabelle more than anything and I've been patient and helpful and kind, I've played my cards right, I've been the perfect guy! I go above and beyond every time! And all I get are these little 'thank you's and 'maybe's and 'I don't drink coffee's!! These little teases, these tiny hints that don't amount to ANYTHING! And it was midnight and we were so drunk—and I balls'd up and I kissed her and she didn't—so I—I am the perfect guy! I deserve her. I've worked so hard, and I deserve her! I'm not the only one who wants this! We all want the same fucking thing, but we make all

163

these excuses; it's too soon, it's not right, blah, blah, blah—
and we're all expected to suppress the most natural thing
in the world! And you know, maybe we— aren't supposed
to! Maybe this is what happens when you come too far!! We
try to suppress these—biological things, but . . . we all want
things we can't have! And that's everyone! But men are the
ones with the power to take what they want! *We* have to carry that burden! We have to snuff that out every day and if it
comes out at the wrong fucking time, we're held responsible.

RIGHTS AND PERMISSIONS

AFTER © 2019 by Michael McKeever. Reprinted by permission of the author. For performance rights, contact Barbara Hogenson, Hogenson Agency, bhogenson@aol.com.

AMERICAN SON © 2015 by Christopher Demos Brown. Reprinted by permission of Ali Tesluk, Samuel French, Inc. For performance rights, contact Samuel French, Inc., 212-206-8990, www.samuelfrench.com.

ANARCHY © 2017 by Don Nigro. Reprinted by permission of Don Nigro. For performance rights, contact Samuel French, Inc., 212-206-8990, www.samuelfrench.com.

THE ANTELOPE PARTY © 2018 by Eric John Meyer. Reprinted by permission of the author. For performance rights, contact Broadway Play Publishing, 212-772-8334, www.broadwayplaypubl.com.

ASKING FOR IT © 2019 by Molly Goforth. Reprinted by permission of the author. For performance rights, contact Molly Goforth, mollyegoforth@gmail.com.

ATLAS PIT © 2015 by Alex Paul Burkart. Reprinted by permission of Peregrine Whittlesey, Peregrine Whittlesey Agency. For performance rights, contact Peregrine Whittlesey, pwwagy@aol.com.

AT ST. WILDING'S © 2019 by Monica Raymond. Reprinted by permission of the author. For performance rights, contact Monica Raymond, femmevox@hotmail.com.

AT THE TABLE © 2019 Michael Perlman. Reprinted by permission of Amy Wagner, Abrams Artists Agency. For performance rights, contact Amy Wagner, amy.wagner@abramsartny.com.

BABEL © 2019 by Jacquelyn Goldfinger. Reprinted by permission of Amy Wagner, Abrams Artists Agency. For performance rights, contact Amy Wagner, amy.wagner@abramsartny.com.

BERNHARDT/HAMLET © 2018 by Madwoman in the Attic, Inc.. Reprinted by permission of Scott Falk, ICM Partners. For performance rights, contact Samuel French, Inc., 212-206-8990, www.samuelfrench.com.

BETWEEN HERE AND DEAD © 2019 by Merridith Allen. Reprinted by permission of the author. For performance rights, contact Merridith Allen, merridith.allen26@gmail.com.

BIG SCARY ANIMALS © 2018 by Matt Lyle. Reprinted by permission of the author. For performance rights, contact Matt Lyle, mattdlyle77@gmail.com.

BOMBER'S MOON © 2019 by Deborah Yarchun. Reprinted by permission of the author. For performance rights, contact Deborah Yarchun, deborah.yarchun@ gmail.com.

BOTTICELLI VENUS © 2017 by Don Nigro. Reprinted by permission of Don Nigro. For performance rights, contact Samuel French, Inc., 212-206-8990, www.samuelfrench.com.

A BRIEF HISTORY OF PENGUINS AND PROMISCUITY © 2017 by James McLindon. Reprinted by permission of the author. For performance rights, contact James McLindon, jmclindon@gmail.com.

BUT WHEN I STARTED TO PLAY © 2019 by Max Baker. Reprinted by permission of the author For performance rights, contact Max Baker, mpbbaker@gmail.com.

CAN'T LIVE WITHOUT YOU © 2019 by Philip Middleton Williams. Reprinted by permission of the author. For performance rights, contact Philip Middleton Williams, pmw@barkbarkwoofwoof.com.

THE CHINESE LADY © 2019 by Lloyd Suh. Reprinted by permission of Beth Blickers, Agency for the Performing Arts. For performance rights, contact Beth Blickers, bblickers@apa-agency.com.

CHURCH & STATE © 2017 by Jason Odell Williams. Reprinted by permission of the author. For performance rights, contact Dramatists Play Service, 212-683-8960.

THE COUPLE NEXT DOOR © 2010 by Donna Hoke. Reprinted by permission of the author. For performance rights, contact Donna Hoke, donna@donnahoke.com.

DEAD MOVEMENT © 2018 by John Patrick Bray. Reprinted by permission of the author. For performance rights, contact John Patrick Bray, johnpatrickbray@ gmail.com.

(DON'T) LOOK AT ME © 2018 by Molly Goforth. Reprinted by permission of the author. For performance rights, contact Molly Goforth, mollyegoforth@gmail .com.

DOWNTOWN RACE RIOT © 2019 by Seth Zvi Rosenfeld. Reprinted by permission of Olivier Sultan, Creative Artists Agency. For performance rights, contact Olivier Sultan, osultan@caa.com.

THE DRAMA DEPARTMENT © 2019 by James Hindman. Reprinted by permission of the author. For performance rights, contact James Hindman, seidojim@aol .com.

EDUCATION © 2018 by Brian Dykstra. Reprinted by permission the author. For performance rights, contact Brian Dykstra, briandykstra@earthlink.net.

ENTERPRISE © 2018 by Brian Parks. Reprinted by permission of the author. For performance rights, contact Brian Parks, bparks3000@yahoo.com.